I Ching
for Serious
Beginners

Rosemary Howell

First published May 1996

Reprinted October 1996

© *1996 Chatelaine Publishing cc*

P.O.Box 23447

Claremont

7700

South Africa

ISBN 0-620-20192-4

Since this book is a companion to Wilhelm's Book of Changes, he has been liberally quoted throughout. The edition used was the Routledge, Kegan Paul Edition . The Book of Changes is presently published by Penguin/Arkana.

Set in 11pt. Times Roman

Printed and bound by FormsXpress, Cape Town, South Africa

Contents

"Our deepest fear is not that we are inadequate. Our deepest fear is that we are powerful beyond measure. It is our light, not our darkness, that most frightens us. We ask ourselves, who am I to be brilliant, gorgeous, talented and fabulous? Actually, who are you not to be? You are a child of God. Your playing small doesn't serve the world. There is nothing enlightened about shrinking so that other people won't feel insecure around you.

We are born to make manifest the glory of God that is within us. It's not just in some of us; it's in everyone.

And as we let our own light shine, we unconsciously give other people permission to do the same. As we are liberated from our own fear, our presence automatically liberates others."

Marianne Williamson
"A Return to Love"

Dedication

This book is lovingly written for my teacher Iris Knight who herself was dedicated to lecturing and teaching this philosophy. She has proved such a worthy guardian of it all her life and richly deserves recognition.

For my late husband, broadcaster Henry Howell, who was the epitome of the I Ching's philosophy and encouraged me to write this book.

to all my students past and present who asked me to put my teachings onto paper;

and to all those earnestly seeking a Truth.

but especially is it dedicated to the spirit of **I CHING**

Preface

When one has the rare pleasure of meeting Rosemary Howell, one is struck by a sense of timelessness and pure spirit. One instinctively knows that Rosemary began her spiritual quest the day she was born. Through what she terms "an unusual childhood" growing up in wartime England under the care of a loving Victorian grandmother, she was drawn to the symbolism and pageantry of the Catholic convent she was sent to at the age of four. Her later request to become a nun was wisely refused by her grandmother who could clearly see that Rosemary had a different path to follow.

Rosemary has an exact and questioning mind, a beguiling sense of humour and could be called a spiritual detective. Her extensive search for hidden meanings in religions and philosophies led her down many avenues and ultimately to the I Ching. She herself is a lady of subtle change so the fact that she has studied the Book of Changes for almost 25 years comes as no surprise at all.

Rosemary knows from sources deep within her that she will always be a student of the I Ching. "One always is – we cannot ever fully know it." It has never once failed to challenge her and it is these challenges that she passes on to other students in her workshops and now through this book.

For Rosemary the I Ching is a tool through which her Higher Self finds expression and a Path from which she will not deviate. In her next book on the I Ching, Rosemary intends to uncover, with the aid of some rather unusual team-mates, the answers to questions all thinking humans have pondered for most of their lives.

The rather unusual team-mates referred to are extraterrestrials who first contacted her at an early age. In her own words, she is "out of the closet now" and can speak freely of her experiences. When she was seven she was lovingly lifted into a space craft hovering just above her secret tree house. "I felt no fear; it didn't enter my head – it seemed quite natural. I remember sitting on someone's lap in front of a computer-type console and exclaiming about 'the pretty lights!' No wonder I'm addicted to my computer." She was told, among other things, that she would have a difficult haul for the next fifty years — and she certainly did. But they assured her they would be near her always, that she was of their family and within those fifty years would experience sightings and telepathic contact. This experience was erased from her memory. Then in 1969 she had an awe-inspiring sighting, with witnesses, and direct communication. Then when she was 57 life began to straighten out dramatically and she is "where I want to be, doing what I am meant to be doing".

Rosemary is also the South African correspondent for Quest International's UFO Magazine. As such she promotes and researches UFO-related information —sightings and so-called abductions — and holds regular meetings to disseminate and gather information. On the subject of abductions she says, "I feel that word is questionable. I believe prior agreements were made with our space brothers and sisters but the memory of this agreement is hidden deep within our subconscious, hence the frequent fear. Once we raise our level of consciousness and understanding, this fear dissipates. Then by moving into an altered state of consciousness direct contact can be made – in love and harmony." Rosemary welcomes interaction with other people who have had similar experiences beyond the boundaries of accepted reality.

At this point Rosemary wishes to pay tribute to Tony Dodd, Quest International's Director of Investigations, and renowned as one of the world's foremost investigators. As an ex-policeman he has his feet firmly planted on the ground. When she made contact with him 2 years ago there was an instant rapport and affinity. Since that time he has maintained close personal contact, never failing to explain to her the meaning of her experiences as they occur and the Path she is on. He works tirelessly despite threats made against him. She treasures his faxes, his time, his insights and their friendship.

Following her own telepathic development, Rosemary looked to America for more information. Through the Internet she discovered Lyssa Royal – internationally acclaimed author, lecturer and channel. They became friends. The result was a visit to Cape Town at the beginning of this year by Lyssa Royal and her husband Ronald Lee

Holt, hosted by Rosemary who organised various workshops for Lyssa. "It gave me great joy to be able to share this incredible lady's talents and knowledge with others", says Rosemary. "I was particularly happy to organise a young people's workshop. It is so important to educate the very young about life elsewhere." She is delighted that Lyssa and Ron Holt are returning to South Africa in September.

Although Rosemary's primary passions are the I Ching and her work as a UFO researcher, she has also written a book called "How to Survive Widowhood and What to Expect". Her most important work to date however, has been a biography of her beloved late husband Henry Howell "A Measure of the Man". This book on "the greatest broadcaster this country had the good fortune to possess" was researched with a thoroughness and dedication which is evident throughout the work. It also covers the history of broadcasting in this country up until 1991, the year which heralded a new era. An updated soft cover edition will be published later this year.

Her I Ching teacher, Iris Knight now 85, says "We have enjoyed a beautifully loving friendship for over 25 years – never a quarrel, always deep affection between us. I have a great love for her, and am proud that this outstanding student has completed this work so well. She has given it depth and love. Thank you, darling girl, for a job well done. I'm very proud."

As anyone who has attempted divination through the I Ching will know, the Book of Changes is at best cryptic. Rosemary has put a great deal of work, thought, experience and research into this companion to Wilhelm. She has kept it simple and concise to help those with a true desire to learn the art. Although I may not subscribe to Rosemary's more out of the ordinary beliefs, I have found working with her a most refreshing experience. It is my hope that students of the I Ching will find this book just as refreshing.

Rachel Topping
Author's Editor

Introduction

The aim of this book is to be a *companion* and *helper* to those persons who seriously wish to begin to learn the I Ching. It is hoped it will also assist those who wish to teach it.

It is intended as a companion to Richard Wilhelm's **'I Ching or Book of Changes'** which was and is the basis of my own studies and work. Wilhelm's interpretation and treatise is considered the bible of this philosophy.

The I Ching is a guide, teacher and sage. It should therefore become a well-thumbed friend!

The ancient Chinese philosophy of the I Ching can be traced back to the 12th Century BC and was studied and used by Confucius, Jung and others. (See Wilhelm.) It is based on the metaphysical concept that there is only **Change**, and that the **Yin/Yang** or **Negative** and **Positive** sides of our nature should be in harmony with each other and with the **Universal Consciousness.** Studying the history, philosophy and psychology of the I Ching will enable the seeker to be a true student, using the knowledge for divination and guidance, personal growth and expansion. Additionally, an in-depth study of the **World of Thought** will reveal the cosmic order behind things.

All these are contained in this book which is a metaphysical approach to the I Ching, to be used in conjunction with Wilhelm.

The additional purpose of this book is to fill a much-needed gap. I have not found one book which fully explains 'the world of thought' i.e. the hexagram behind the present situation; that which is causing, or has caused, it. It is obvious that there are forces at work behind any problem that has arisen – and as man has to imagine a chair before he can design it on paper and bring it into effect, such is the world of thought – vital information to assist in interpreting the I Ching's advice.

Chapter 1
Brief Historical Background
Basic Principles
Sequence of the Eight Trigrams

First we will look at a little of the origin of the I Ching and then we'll use our imagining factor and travel through time.

The I Ching and its philosophy of change came to light in China in the middle of the 12th Century BC, but it may well have been in use much earlier. However, at the time the House of Yin came to an end, and the House of Chou (King Wen's son) was rising. King Wen and the tyrant Chou Hsin were pitted against each other. Wen lost and he and his son were imprisoned. In prison first the father, then the son, put on to paper the hexagrams and their meanings.[1] It is not known how they were inspired to do this. Originally the lines on the backs of tortoise shells were used by the Sages for divination because the tortoise was esteemed and highly valued. Research reveals that the tortoise is the oldest symbol for planet Earth and the personification of Goddess energy.

Confucius has been credited with some of the interpretations. Carl Jung used the I Ching consistently in his work with the mentally ill. Lourens van der Post was another follower (see Van der Post's 'Jung – a man for our time'). Certainly the I Ching goes back to a time when the holy men found it necessary to look to the heavens/ Universal Consciousness/ God for answers to men's problems on earth.

The basic principle of the I Ching (or Book of Changes) is that of Yin/Yang – Male/Female–Heaven/Earth–Positive/Negative. **Yin** is the feminine principle, **Yang** the male and all things have their being from their catalystic nature. Yin and Yang work together in specific ways to produce specific results.

---

[1] A complete chart of the hexagrams may be found on the inside gatefold of the back cover.

――――――	**YANG** – Creative, heaven, male, father, strong.
――――――	(3 straight lines)
――――――	

―― ――	**YIN** – Receptive, earth, female, mother, gentle.
―― ――	(3 broken lines)
―― ――	

Heaven (Yang) moved downwards to Earth (Yin) who yielded unto him.

YANG the Creative (――――) and YIN the Receptive (―― ――) gave birth to three sons and three daughters – and with them became the eight principles which are the basic trigrams (three-lined 'characters') which in their various configurations form a hexagram 'reading'. The three sons are :

―― ――	
―― ――	**CHEN**: eldest son – THUNDER, arousing, movement
――――――	

―― ――	
――――――	**KAN**: middle son – WATER, abysmal, danger, clouds
―― ――	

――――――	
―― ――	**KEN**: youngest son – MOUNTAIN, keeping still, standstill
―― ――	

Note the dominance of the feminine (broken line) in the males, and that the male (a straight line) moves through three positions within each trigram.

The three daughters are:–

――――――	
――――――	**SUN**: eldest daughter – WIND, gentle, penetrating, wood
―― ――	

```
─────
── ──        LI: middle daughter – FIRE, clinging, light-giving, sun
─────

── ──
─────        TUI: youngest daughter – LAKE, joyous, pleasure
─────
```

Note the predominance of male lines in their female counterparts: they start with a female (broken) line at the base, then move to the centre, and then to the top, in each trigram.

It will be noted that these eight basic trigrams are based on the primary forces of nature. The resulting 64 hexagrams denote all of man's emotional and daily problems, together with advice on how to deal with them. However these pieces of advice are extremely cryptic. Therefore intuition and a quiet mind are necessary prerequisites for casting and interpreting the reading. It is essential to be in a meditative and intuitive frame of mind at all times when approaching the I Ching. The I Ching is a wise, holy and kind friend whose advice one can trust and benefit from. *It deserves the greatest respect.*

The 64 hexagrams will be dealt with later as will advice on the attitude required for successful casting.

The trigrams reflect states of change and behaviour patterns as well as symbols, colours, parts of the body, animals, and so on. These give further depth to the reading and a deeper understanding of the Book of Changes.

The **trigrams** indicate (from the bottom):–

```
─────        Heaven (spiritual nature)
─────        Man          (self)
─────        Earth   (physical nature)
```

The six lines of the **hexagram** mean the same, but are paired:

```
_____ ⎫
         ⎬  Heaven
_____ ⎭
_____ ⎫
         ⎬  Man
_____ ⎭
_____ ⎫
         ⎬  Earth
_____ ⎭
```

So, the top represents Man's higher spiritual self and the bottom his lower or base physical self.

God comes forth in the sign of the **Arousing** (eldest son)
He brings all things to completion in the **Gentle** (eldest daughter)
He causes creatures to perceive each other in **Clinging** (middle daughter)
And they serve one another in **Receptive** (Yin, Mother)
He brings joy in the sign of **Joyous** (youngest daughter)
He battles in the sign of the **Creative** (Yang, Father)
He toils in the sign of **Abysmal** (middle son)
He brings to perfection in **Keeping Still** (youngest son)
In **Arousing** (eldest son) all living things come forth .

In **Gentle** (eldest daughter) they come to completion (pure, perfect)
Clinging (middle daughter) is the brightness in which they all perceive one another
Receptive (Yin, Mother) is the service they all give one another
Joyous (youngest daughter) is mid-Autumn and gives joy to all
In the **Creative** (Yang, Father) dark and light arouse each other
Abysmal (middle son) is water, toil and service
In **Keeping Still** (youngest son) all creatures are perfect.

Of all the forces that **Move** things, none are swifter than **Thunder** (eldest son)
Of all that **Bend** things, none are more able than **Wind** (eldest daughter)
Of all that **Warm**, none are more drying than **Fire** (middle daughter)
Of all that give **Joy**, none are more gladdening than **Lake** (youngest daughter)
Of all that **Moisten**, none are more than **Water** (middle son)

Of all that **End and Begin** things, none are more glorious than **Keeping Still** (youngest son).

Therefore

Fire and **Water** complement (middle son; middle daughter)
Thunder and **Wind** do not interfere (eldest son; eldest daughter)
Mountain and **Lake** are united (youngest son; youngest daughter)

That is to say
only Change and Transformation are possible,
and thus only can all things come to Perfection.
(Wilhelm)

The **Creative** is strong: it's a horse – it's a head
Receptive is yielding: it's a cow or a mare – it's a belly
Arousing is movement: it's a dragon – it's a foot
Gentle is penetrating: it's a cock – it's thighs
Abysmal is dangerous: it's a pig – it's an ear
Clinging is dependence: it's a pheasant – an eye
Keeping Still is standstill: it is a dog – a hand
Joyous is pleasure: a sheep – a mouth

Head **(Creative)** governs the whole body; the belly **(Receptive)** stores up
Foot **(eldest son)** steps on the ground and moves; hand **(youngest son)** holds fast
Thighs **(eldest daughter)** branch downwards; mouth **(youngest daughter)** opens upwards
Ear **(middle son)** is hollow outside; eye **(middle daughter)** is hollow inside

All these are pairs of opposites.

The eight trigrams and their deeper meanings:

CHI'EN – CREATIVE, HEAVEN, MALE ⁣⁣⁣⁣⁣⁣⁣⁣⁣⁣ ———
⁣———
⁣———

Father, round, prince, jade (most precious jewel of China), metal (firm, strong, unyielding), cold, ice, deep red, old horse (reliable), good horse, wild horse, tree and fruit, spotless purity, firm, power, endurance, strength, straight, dragon, upper garment, word.

K'UN – RECEPTIVE, EARTH, FEMALE   — —
                                              — —
                                              — —

Mother, cloth (spread out), kettle (things are cooked until done), earth (the melting pot of life), frugality, level (no partiality), cow and calf (fertile), large wagon (earth carrying all living things), form, multitude, shaft (body of tree from which all branches spring – as all life springs from earth), black soil (black is intensified darkness).

CHEN – AROUSING – eldest son – THUNDER   — —
                                                    — —
                                                    ———

Dragon, dark yellow (mixture of dark heavens and yellow earth), spreading out (blossoming), luxurious growth of Spring covering the earth, a great road (Universal way of life), decisive, vehement, bamboo that is green and young, reed and rush (bamboo, reed and rush are especially fast growing), horses that neigh well (denoting their relationship to thunder), those with white hind legs (gleaming from afar), those which gallop (lively), pod-bearing plants (retaining pods), strong.

SUN – GENTLE – eldest daughter – WIND   ———
                                                   ———
                                                   — —

Wood, guide-line, work, white, long, high, advance and retreat (changeableness), indecision, odour. Among men: grey-haired, elderly, white-haired, those with broad foreheads, with much white in the eyes (associated with arrogance and vehemence). Those eager for gain are also vehement; those close to gain so as to get a three-fold value.Guide-

8

line means windlike dissemination of commands. White is the colour of the Yin principle.

K'AN – ABYSMAL – middle son – WATER

Ditches, ambush, bending and straightening out, bow and wheel, melancholy men, those with sick hearts and earache; blood sign, red; horses with beautiful backs, with wild courage, letting heads hang, with thin hoofs, stumbling; chariots with many defects; penetration, the moon, thieves; wood that is firm with much pith (associated with penetration), toil, pains in ear from laborious listening, blood as fluid of the body (but brighter than the red of the Creative), people who secretly penetrate a place and sneak away as thieves.

LI – CLINGING – middle daughter – FIRE

Coats of mail, helmets, lances, weapons, big-bellied among men, dryness, tortoise, crab, snail, mussel, trees which dry out in the upper part of the trunk; firm without and hollow within.

K'EN – KEEPING STILL – youngest son – MOUNTAIN

Bypath, little stones, doors and openings, fruits and seeds, eunuchs and watchmen, fingers, dog, rat, black-billed birds (grip things easily), firm and gnarled trees because they possess great powers of resistance, fruit and seeds are the link between the end and the beginning. Eunuchs are doorkeepers – watchmen guard the streets; both watch and protect. Fingers hold fast, a dog guards, a rat gnaws.

TUI – JOYOUS – youngest daughter – LAKE   — —
                                                      ——
                                                      ——

Sorceress (woman who speaks), mouth and tongue, dropping off and bursting open, smashing and breaking apart, hard and salty soil (where lakes have dried up), concubine, sheep (outwardly weak, inwardly stubborn).

Chapter 2
The Philosophy of Change
Judgements and Lines

In the I Ching a philosophical distinction is drawn between the different kinds of change.

Non-change is the background against which change is made possible. In any change there is a fixed point to which the change can be referred otherwise there is no definite order, only chaos. This point of reference must be established and always requires a **choice** and a **decision** (based on the philosophy that at the dawn of consciousness one stood already enclosed within pre-potent (more powerful than others) systems of relationships.

The problem is to choose one's point of reference so that it coincides with the point of reference for cosmic events. Only then can the world created by one's decision escape being dashed to pieces against pre-potent systems of relationships with which it would otherwise come into conflict. The premise for such a decision is the belief that in the final analysis the world is a system of homogenous relationships – that is, order not chaos.

The ultimate frame of reference for all that changes is the non-changing.

The two cardinal principles of all existence are symbolised in the two fundamental hexagrams **CREATIVE** and **RECEPTIVE**. They are not a dualism but are united by a relationship based on homogeneity: they do not conflict, but complement each other (male/female – a catalyst from which other things flow.) This difference in energy level creates a potential by which movement and living expressions of energy become possible.

In the heavens constant movement and change prevail.

On earth apparently fixed and lasting conditions prevail. This is a delusion of course; nothing is regarded as absolutely at rest. Rest is merely an intermediate state of movement or latent movement. However, there are points at which the movement becomes visible, symbolised by the fact that the hexagrams are built up from both firm and yielding lines. The firm and strong indicate the principle of movement, the yielding a principle of rest. Firm is undivided – light, yang; yielding is broken – dark, yin.

Because the character of the firm combines with the character of the place, a great multiplicity of possible situations result. This serves to symbolise a third link of events in the world. There are conditions of equilibrium (harmony) prevailing, and conditions of disturbed equilibrium (confusion).

There is a system of order pervading the whole world and when each is in its appropriate place harmony is established, as can be seen in nature. Things move by order, and by forces impacting on them from the outside. It is therefore not possible for harmony to be attained under all circumstances. Deviations may occur bringing confusion and disorder. In the human sphere harmony assures good fortune; disharmony predicts misfortune – all represented by a combination of lines and places in the I Ching.

Phenomena take place in the heavens and obey definite laws. Bound up with them, forms come into being on earth in accordance with identical laws. If we know the laws of change we can pre-calculate accordingly and freedom of action therefore becomes possible.

The purpose of the I Ching is to demonstrate the laws by means of the laws of change operating in the respective hexagrams. Once we can reproduce these laws, we acquire a comprehensive view of events; we can understand the past and future equally well and bring this knowledge to bear in our actions. Therefore the eight trigrams succeed each other by turns, as the firm and yielding displace each other. This rotation of phenomena each succeeding the other until the starting point is reached again is known as **Cyclic Change.** Cyclic change is the recurrent change in the organic world.

Sequent Change is the progressive (non-recurrent) change of phenomena produced by causality (no turning back). The firm and yielding displace each other within the eight trigrams. The firm is transformed and becomes the yielding; the yielding changes and becomes the firm. In this way the eight trigrams change from one into another in turn, and the regular alternation of the phenomena within the year takes its course.

There are two directions of movement –

Descending	Ascending
Ch'ien	K'un

- Creative
- Heaven
- Male
- Yang

- Receptive
- Earth
- Female
- Yin

In the changing seasons of the year each trigram is the cause of the next.

… deep in the womb of earth stirs the creative force (**Arousing**). An electrical force appears and discharges itself (**Lightning**). Thunder is put before lightning as it is considered to be the agent evoking the lightning. Then **Wind** (Thunder's opposite) sets in. Wind brings rain – then there is a shift. Lightning and rain move to their primary forms as sun and moon causing heat and cold cyclically. When the sun is at its zenith it causes heat. This is shown by the **Joyous Lake**. When moon is at its zenith, cold sets in. This is shown by the **Mountain** (Keeping Still).

The way of the Creative brings about the male; the way of the Receptive the female. This indicates sequent change manifested in the succession of the generations, never returning to its starting point.

The **Creative** knows the great beginning; the **Receptive** produces the finished things. The **Creative** produces the invisible seeds of all development. At first they are purely abstract – no action – in a state of being created (or germinated).This is the world of invisible movement which is effortless. The **Receptive** acts on matter in space and time and brings material things to completion. It is repose, it is the germ of all spatial diversity.

'.....what is easy is easy to know, what is simple is easy to follow. He who is easy to know attains fealty (fidelity); he who is easy to follow attains works. He who possesses attachment (by others) can endure for long; he who possesses works can become great. To endure is the disposition of the Sage; greatness is the field of action of the Sage.'

In other words in human life the simple and easy take effect as given above. What is easy is readily understood and from this comes its power of suggestion. He whose ideas are clear and is easily understood wins men's adherence because he embodies love. He becomes free of confusing conflicts and disharmonies. The same applies in the realm of action.

Briefly then the hexagrams are representatives of earthly phenomena. As the firm and yielding lines displace one another so change and transformation arise. Therefore good fortune and misfortune are the images of gain and loss; remorse and humiliation the images of sorrow and forethought.

The judgement 'remorse' is an exhortation to feel sorrow and turn back. 'Humiliation' is the exhortation when a given trend was right at the start, but arrogance has set in. It indicates a slipping from good to bad fortune. Therefore exercise forethought, check yourself, and turn back to good fortune.

'Misfortune' means that the trend is in opposition to the laws of the Universe.

Because the Book of Changes reaches down to the regions of the unconscious/ subconscious, Space (diversity and confusion), and Time (uncertainty) are eliminated by the deep and the simple, and by the easy (the germinal). Change and transformation are images of progress and retrogression. Therefore a superior man (meaning a wise and sensible person) devotes himself to that from which he attains tranquillity. It is the judgement on the individual lines that the superior man takes pleasure in and ponders on. Therefore we shape our lives according to the ideas in the Book which is a reproduction of all existing conditions. Life in its turn will become a reproduction of this Law of Change.

Sincere students of the I Ching believe that people want to be spiritual, healthy, kind and intelligent, to be responsible for assisting others to reach the same level of achievement, and to enjoy the truth. Additionally, it is believed that for synchronicity to be at work and understood, it is essential that the moment of synchronicity be seized, be worked with by seeking advice in any doubtful situation and thus used to our advantage and for our growth. *Right action keeps us on our intended Path.*

The Book of Changes embraces the essential meaning of the various situations of life; thus we are in a position to shape our lives meaningfully, by acting in accordance with order and sequence, and doing in each case what is appropriate to the situation. We are then equal to every situation because we do not resist the I Ching's meaning and thus obtain peace of soul. Our actions are set in order and the mind is satisfied.

When we meditate on the judgements of each individual line we intuitively perceive the inter-relationships in the world. During meditation consider the judgements and obtain wisdom therefrom. During action consult the oracle and follow its directions accordingly.

King Wen's judgements (decisions) refer always to the situation in the hexagram as a whole. The judgements appended by his son, the Duke of Chou, to the individual lines refer in each instance to the changes taking place within this situation. Decisions refer to the images; judgements on the lines refer to the changes. These judgements on a line are to be considered **only** when the cast lines move, i.e. a **6** or a **9.**

'Good Fortune'	gain
'Misfortune'	loss
'Remorse' or 'Humiliation'	minor imperfections
'No blame'	one can rectify one's mistakes in the right way.

Therefore the classification of superior and inferior is based on the individual places; the equalising of great and small is based on the hexagrams and the discrimination between good fortune and misfortune is based on the judgements.

In the hexagram itself, King Wen gave appropriately named positions to each line – and used a King and his officials as examples. However the lowest and top lines are outside the situation. The lowest is inferior because it has not yet entered the situation, or is just entering the situation raised by the querant. The topmost is superior – the place of the Sage no longer involved in worldly affairs (or an eminent man without power), or is moving out of the situation in question.

Of the inner places, the 2nd and 4th lines are those of officials, or sons, or women. (The 4th is higher, the 2nd inferior to it.) The 3rd and 5th are places of authority; the 3rd because it is the top line of the lower trigram, and the 5th because it is the place of the ruling line (and ruler) of the hexagram. The 3rd and 4th lines also indicate the present 'field of action' (what is happening now).

'Great' signifies a firm line; 'Small' signifies a yielding line. They are equalised in the hexagram as a whole. Both can be favourable and indicate good fortune when in their proper places. If to yield in a situation is advantageous, a yielding line in a yielding place will be particularly favourable. The same applies to a firm. If strength is required, then a firm place is more advantageous for a yielding line. *Remember*: The commentary on the moving lines indicates in which direction the situation is developing.

The Book of Changes contains the measure of heaven and earth, therefore it enables us to comprehend the tao/path/movement of heaven and earth and its order.

It presents a complete image of heaven and earth; a microcosm of all possible relationships and enables us to calculate the movements in every situation to which they apply. One can investigate the laws of the universe and obtain ultimate mastery of 'fate'.

Looking upwards we contemplate, with its help, the signs in the heavens. Looking down we examine the lines of the earth. Thus we come to know the circumstances of the dark and the light. Going back to the beginning of things and pursuing them to the end we come to know the lessons of birth and death. The union of seed and power produces all things; the escape of the soul brings about change. Through this we come to know the conditions of outgoing and returning spirits.

The hexagrams are constructed from the elements of the two basic principles of dark and light – Yin and Yang. The individual lines are either at rest or in motion. When at rest (7) or yielding (8) they build up the hexagram. When in motion the 9 (firm, big Yang) or the 6 (yielding, big Yin) break down the hexagram to transform it into a new hexagram. These are the processes that open our eyes to the secrets of life.

We know that birth and death are not absolutes any more than the changes of the seasons within the year are. Just as the resting lines of hexagrams build up and produce change when they begin to move, so bodily existence is built up by the union of 'outgoing' life streams of seed (male) with power (female).

This corporeal existence remains relatively constant as long as the constructive forces are in the resting state: in equilibrium. When they begin to move, the psychic element escapes (upward), the lower sinks to the earth: disintegration. The spiritual forces that produce the building up and breaking down of visible existence likewise belong either to the light or dark principle. The light spirits (Shen) are outgoing – active – entering on new incarnations. The dark (Kei) return home – withdrawing forces assimilating what life has yielded; the ebb and flow of the great ocean of life.

Since in this way Man resembles heaven and earth he is not in conflict with them. His wisdom embraces all things and his tao (essence) brings order to the whole world. Therefore he does not err. He is active everywhere but does not let himself be carried away. He rejoices in heaven, has knowledge of fate and is free of care. When content with his circumstances, genuine in his kindness, he can practice love.

Man is made up of four propositions based on wisdom and love, justice and mores (ethics) – which are the four basics of hexagram 1 – The Creative: 'sublime success; perseverance furthers.' The effect of wisdom, love and justice is shown in the first proposition. On the basis of all-embracing wisdom, the regulations springing from a love of the world can be so shaped that all goes well for everyone and no mistakes are made. This is what furthers.

Man should exude wisdom and love excluding no person or thing, regulated by the mores which do not allow one to be carried away into anything improper or one-sided, and therefore have success.

Man should enjoy harmony of mind, perfect in wisdom, that rejoices in heaven and understands its dispensations; this provides the basis for perseverance.

Man should show the love that acquiesces trustingly in every situation and, out of its store of inner kindness, manifests itself in goodwill to all men, thereby attaining sublimity – the root of all good.

The reason we can obtain mastery over fate is because reality is always conditioned, and these conditions of time and space limit and determine it. The spirit, however, is not bound by these conditions and can bring them about as its own purposes require.

The Book is so widely applicable because it contains only these purely spiritual relationships which are so abstract they can find expression within every framework of reality. They contain only the tao that underlies events. Therefore all chance contingencies can be shaped according to this tao. The conscious applications of these possibilities assure mastery over fate.

That which lets the dark appear and now the light is Tao. It is that which becomes mobile and maintains the interplay of forces.

The cycle of change is represented in circular form in the Primal Beginning. It is the Yin/Yang symbol, also known as 't'ai chi t'u.' This is a symbol that has played a vital role in Chinese thought. The dark side (yin, feminine, left side of the body) has within it a spot of light indicating that in all negativity there is a seed of the positive light force, or 'good'. The light side (yang, masculine, right side of the body) has a dark spot indicating that within positivity/good there is potential for negativity/evil.

The cycle of the primal powers continues uninterruptedly and without end because there rises again and again a state of tension, a potential that keeps them in motion and causes them to unite, thus constantly regenerating. Tao does this without ever becoming manifest. The power of Tao to do this is called 'good.' It is the power that completes things, the power that lends them their individuality and gives them a centre around which they organise. Tao is called the essence – that with which things are endowed at their origin.

The kind man discovers it and calls it kind. People use it day by day and are not aware of it, for the way of the superior man is rare. Tao reveals itself differently to each individual according to his own nature. It gives life to all things. Its glorious power, its great field of action, are of all things the most sublime. It possesses everything in complete abundance – this is its great field of action. It renews everything daily – this is its glorious power. It is omnipresent; everything that exists, in and through it. It renews everything; each day the world is as glorious as the first day of creation.

As the begetter of all begetting it is called **CHANGE**. As that which completes the primal images it is called the **CREATIVE**. As that which initiates them it is called the **RECEPTIVE**. There energy, here matter.

As that which serves for exploring the laws of numbers and thus for knowing the future, it is called **REVELATION**. In that it serves to infuse an organic coherence into the changes it is called the **WORK**. That aspect of it which cannot be fathomed in terms of the light and the dark is called **SPIRIT** (the 'why' which cannot be answered – **TAO**). This then is the I Ching's Philosophy.

The Book of Changes **correctly used** leads to harmony with the ultimate principles of the Universe. The Sages exalted their natures by acquiring the wisdom preserved in the Book.

Heaven and Earth determine the scene and the changes take effect within it. The perfected nature of man, sustaining itself and enduring, is the gateway of Tao and Justice (light and dark), exalting and broadening man's nature.

Confucius said: 'Is not the Book of Changes supreme? By means of it, the holy sages exalted their natures and extended their field of action. Wisdom exalts. The mores make humble. The exalted imitate heaven. The humble follow the example of the earth.' Confucius also said that if he had fifty more years of life, it would not have been enough to study the I Ching. In my small, simple way I can only humbly agree.

(Based on a thesis written in 1979)

Chapter 3
The Construction of a Hexagram
Explaining the Images

The Creative produces quality; the Receptive produces quantity. Because of the vastness (quantity) and greatness (quality) there is correspondence with heaven and earth. Because of changes and continuity there is correspondence with the four seasons. Because of the meaning of light and dark there is correspondence with the sun and the moon. Because of the good in the easy and simple there is correspondence with the supreme power.

Light	yang
Sun	t'ai yang (great light)
Dark	yin
Moon	t'ai yin (great dark)

Line 6 – A sage who has left the world, this line is moving out of the situation. It is effect, not cause. It is Akashic records, karma, the raising of the Kundalini; an ebbing influence.

Line 5 – This is the middle of the primary hexagram, usually favourable. It is the ruling line. It is the place where the situation bears full fruit and signs of decadence are not yet manifest.

Line 4 – This is the place of the Minister, but because it is near the ruler caution must be exercised.

Line 3 – This is insecure, between two primaries. An unfortunate position. It shows the weakness and danger in a situation. It is a firm line of lower rank and therefore limited.

Line 2 – This is the middle of a primary and there usually favourable. It is the official in the provinces who is far from the ruler and does not have to be as cautious as the 4th line. But he advances himself little and works on detail. It is often thorny and full of difficulties.

Line 1 – This has not yet entered the situation to any extent. It is cause not effect. A situation in itself favourable, it can reveal unfavourable aspects when embryonic.

The Images

The Images in the Book were developed from the holy sages surveying all the confused diversities under heaven. They observed forms and phenomena.

The holy sages were able to survey all the movements under heaven. They contemplated the way in which these movements met and became interrelated, to take their course according to eternal laws. They then appended judgements to distinguish between the good fortune and bad fortune indicated – the moving lines.

They observed before they spoke and discussed before they moved. Through observation and discussion they perfected the changes and transformations. The observations of the Image gives us knowledge of the diversity of things; the discussion in the Judgement gives us knowledge of the directions of movements.

The simple is the root of diversity in form (in conformity with the Receptive); the easy is the root of all movement (in conformity with the Creative).

The following extract from Wilhelm's Book of Changes is an example:

> *'A crane calling in the shade. It's young answers it. I have a good goblet; I will share it with you.'*

The Master said: The superior/wise man (the crane) abides in his room (the shade). If his words are well spoken, he meets with assent at a distance of more than 1000 miles. His young (those in agreement) answer him. How much more then from nearby! If the superior man abides in his room and his words are **not** well spoken, he meets with contradiction at a distance of more than 1000 miles! How much more, then, from nearby. Words go forth from one's own person and exert their influence on men. Deeds are born close at hand and become visible far away. Words and deeds are the hinge and bowspring of the superior man. As hinge and bowspring move, they bring honour or disgrace.

Through words and deeds the superior man moves heaven and earth. Must one not, then, be cautious? On a more modern note: a questing gentleman asked me how he should cope with a certain job opportunity he had been offered. The I Ching threw up this particular line. Our understanding was that 'the crane' was the new opportunity – it was 'in the shade', not yet an event; the young who answers it was the questioner, and that 'the good goblet to share' would be the new position. The outcome was excellent, and the gentleman concerned moved to his new post and was highly successful. **Example**

Hexagram 6: Inner Truth – 9 in the 2nd place: on the subject of speaking:

'Men bound in fellowship must first weep and lament, but afterwards they laugh.'

The Master said: Life leads the thoughtful man on a path of many windings. Now the course is checked, now it runs straight again. Here winged thoughts may pour freely forth in words, there the heavy burden of knowledge must be shut away in silence. But when two people are one in their inmost hearts, they shatter even the strength of iron or of bronze. And when two people understand each other in their inmost hearts, their words are sweet and strong, like the fragrance of orchids. (Wilhelm)

Comparison

Hexagram 13 (T'ung Jen) Fellowship with men – 9 in the 5th place: on the subject of speaking: 'To spread white rushes underneath. No blame.'

The Master said: It does well enough simply to place something on the floor. But if one puts white rushes underneath, how could that be a mistake? This is the extreme of caution. Rushes in themselves are worthless, but can have a very important effect. If one is as cautious as this in all that one does, one remains free of mistakes.

A hexagram is made up of two trigrams. The eight trigrams are the primaries of a hexagram. In a hexagram, the lower trigram is called 'inner' (**lower**); the upper is called 'outer' (**upper**). When we go further and add their transitions to the situation, all possible situations on earth are encompassed.

Each of the sixty-four hexagrams can change into another through the appropriate movements of one or more lines. Thus there is *a total of 4096 transitional stages and variations (64x64)*, and these represent every possible situation.

The Book reveals Tao and renders nature and action divine. Therefore with its help we can meet everything in the right way, and with its help can even assist the gods themselves.

In other words it reveals the meaning of events in the Universe and thereby imparts a divine mystery to the nature and action of the man who puts his trust in it. In this way he is able to meet every event in the right/appropriate way, and even to aid the gods in governing the world.

The Master said: whoever knows the tao of the changes and transformations, knows the action of the gods. And here we can realise that we can in no way influence the coins to fall in certain variations out of 4096 options – it would be impossible. Furthermore, when one considers that within a cast hexagram the lines can enjoy a variation of any one line singly or with another, there are a further 21 options.

Chapter 4
The Psychology of the Oracle
Locked and Nuclear Hexagrams

The Book of Changes contains the fourfold tao of the holy sages –

- In speaking, we should be guided by its judgement;

- In action, guided by its changes;

- In making objects, guided by its images;

- In seeking an oracle, guided by its pronouncements.

Therefore the superior man, whenever he has a need to make or do something, consults the Changes and does so in words. It takes up his communications like an echo and thus he learns of the things of the future.

Confucius, he say: **If this Book was not one of the most spiritual things on earth, how could it do this?**

This is the basis of the Oracle: The problem is formulated **precisely** in words and we receive the appropriate oracle which enables us to know the future. This rests on the assumption that the conscious and superconscious enter into a relationship. The conscious process stops with the formulation of the question; the unconscious starts with the casting of the coins. When we compare the results of this casting with the text of the Book we obtain the Oracle.

If one proceeds through the Changes they complete the forms of heaven and earth. If the Changes are followed through to the ultimate they determine all images on earth.

Confucius, he say: **If this were not the most changing thing on earth, how could it do this?**

The Changes have no consciousness and no action. They are quiescent and do not move. But if they are stimulated they penetrate all situations under heaven.

The Changes are what has enabled the holy sages to reach all depths and to grasp the seeds of all things. Only through what is deep can one penetrate all wills on earth. Only through the seeds can one complete all affairs on earth. Only through the divine can one hurry without haste and reach the goal without walking. Here, then, it is shown that because the Book of Changes reaches down into the regions of the unconscious, both Space and Time are eliminated. Space, as the principle of diversity and confusion, is overcome by the deep, the simple. Time as the principle of uncertainty is overcome by the germinal, the easy.

What do the Changes do? They disclose things, complete affairs and encompass all things on earth; this and nothing else. For this reason the holy sages used them to penetrate all wills on earth, to determine all fields of action on earth and to settle all doubts on earth.

The nature of the coins is round and spiritual. The nature of the hexagrams is square and wise. The meaning of the six lines changes in order to furnish information.

The holy sages purified their hearts, withdrew, and hid themselves in secret. They concerned themselves with good fortune and misfortune. They were divine and thus understood the future; they were wise and stored up the past. Only the reason and clear-mindedness of the ancients, their knowledge and wisdom, their unremitting divine power, could have done this. For us to achieve the same heights we must emulate them.

Penetration of all wills is paralleled with the spirituality of the coins. They are round because they are symbols of heaven and of the spirit. The hexagrams stand for earth; their basic number is eight, a total of sixty-four. They serve to determine the field of action.

Finally, the individual lines are moveable and changeable (9 and 6) in order to give information, and to settle doubts pertaining to particular situations. The holy sages possessed this knowledge. They withdrew into seclusion and cultivated the spirit so that they were able to penetrate the minds of all men (penetration); so they could determine good and bad fortune (the field of action); so they knew the past and future (settlement of doubts). They could do this due to their reason and clear-mindedness (penetration of wills), their knowledge and wisdom (determining the fields of action), and their divine power (settlement of doubts). This divine power acts without weakening itself.

Understanding of the Book of Changes calls for similar concentration and meditation.

Therefore they called the closing of the gate the Receptive, the opening of the gate the Creative. The alternation of this closing and opening they called Change. The going backward and forward without ceasing they called Penetration. What manifests itself visibly they called an Image; what has bodily form they called a Tool. What is established in Image is called a Pattern. That which furthers (grows) on going out and coming in, that which all men live by, they called the Divine.

This passage shows the Tao of heaven and the conditions of men. The closing and opening (of gates) signifies the alternation of rest and movement. Penetration is also the state in which the individual has attained sovereign mastery in the psychic sphere.

Therefore there is in the Changes the Great Primal Beginning. This generates the two primary forces. The two primary forces generate the eight images. The eight images generate the eight trigrams. The eight trigrams generate sixty-four hexagrams.

	Great Primal Beginning	
YIN		**YANG**
	Eight Images	
	Eight Trigrams	
	Sixty-four Hexagrams	

The Book says –

> He is blessed by heaven.
> Good fortune.
> Nothing that does not further.

The Master said: To bless means to help. Heaven helps the man who is devoted. Men help the man who is true. He who walks in truth and is devoted in his thinking, and reveres the worthy, is blessed by heaven. He has good fortune; and there is nothing that would not further.

The Creative and the Receptive are the **real** secret of the changes. Inasmuch as the Creative and Receptive present themselves as complete, the changes between them are also posited. If the Creative and Receptive were destroyed there would be nothing by which the changes could be perceived. If there were no more changes to be seen the effects of the Creative and Receptive would also gradually cease. Life depends on the polarity between activity and receptivity. This maintains tension, every adjustment of which manifests itself as a change, a process of life. These tensions too are constantly being generated anew by the changes inherent in life.

That which transforms things and fits them together is called **change**. That which stimulates them and sets them in motion is called **continuity**. That which raises them up and sets them forth is called the **field of action.**

Summary

The Changes is a book from which one may not hold aloof. Its Tao is forever changing. Alteration, movement without rest, flowing through the six lines. Rising and sinking without fixed law the firm and the yielding transform each other. They cannot be confined within a rule. It is only **Change** that is at work here. They move inward and outward according to fixed rhythms. Without or within they teach caution. They also show care and sorrow and their causes. Although you have no teacher, approach them as you would your parents. First take up the words, ponder their meaning, then the fixed rules reveal themselves. But if you are not the right (diligent) man the meaning will not manifest itself to you.

The Changes is a book whose hexagrams begin with the first line and are summed up in the last. The lines are the essential material. The beginning and top lines stand in relationship to cause and effect. Judgement on the first line is tentative but everything attains completion in the last. But if one wishes to explore things in their manifold gradation, and their qualities as well, and to discriminate between right and wrong, it cannot be done completely without the middle lines (the fields of action.)

One could also say that the first (bottom) line (if cast) is coming into the situation, or possibly has just happened. The third and fourth lines (if cast) are the here and now of the situation (the field of action), the second and fifth are rulers and very favourable, and the sixth (top) is moving outside the situation. The top line is invariably negative (with a few exceptions), in keeping with the concept that if we have reached a point where a question needs to be asked then change is about to take place. Thus negativity is moving out of the situation and any other moving lines will explain in more detail what is actually happening, or how we should deal with the problem.

Locked Hexagrams

If all the lines cast are 7s (young yang) and 8s (young yin) there are obviously no moving lines. This is called a 'locked' or static hexagram. There is no outcome, no specific advice. The I Ching is telling us that the situation is fraught with danger or tension and that nothing should be done – certainly not by the person for whom the question has been asked. However, one can (depending on the nature of the question) revise the wording of the question in order to ascertain what can be done, and by whom.

In most instances all the lines can be read and each one will describe the situation the querant has found himself in, but they are **not** to be followed as guidance. They serve as an explanation. Note: A locked hexagram does not always infer that no action should be taken. It could be answering 'yes, but not now'.

Example

Miss Y had been invited to travel overseas on a friend's yacht. She asked "Shall (Miss Y) travel overseas on Mr X's yacht?" Answer: locked hexagram 53 – gradual progress to union. Because she had not given a time to go the I Ching answered literally "No not today." But it was obvious from hexagram 53 that she *would* go. The interpretation is quite clearly 'yes, in due course'.

Nuclear Trigrams

Lines 2, 3 and 4 would become the three lines of the lower hexagram, and lines 3, 4 and 5 would become the three lines of the upper hexagram – giving a new hexagram which is called the 'nuclear'. This is the 'heart of the matter' of the present (first cast) hexagram, and gives more information about the circumstances surrounding the present situation. Interestingly, if one were to work the nuclears out one from another, the 64th nuclear hexagram would be the one you first started with!

It is not recommended that you work with more than one present-time nuclear; it can become very confusing, bearing in mind that the I Ching knows everything and is giving a poor simple human being far more information than he could possibly hope to cope with or understand. One nuclear is enough. A nuclear trigram is taken from a current (1 - 64) hexagram thus –

Of the six lines, drawn, for example, like this:

```
— —
— — ⎤ this would        — —
———— ⎥ be the upper
———— ⎦ trigram          ————
— —
— —
```

```
— —
— —
————  ⎤ this would be          ————
————  ⎥ the lower             ————
— —   ⎦ trigram              — —
— —
```

The guiding lines can be read from a nuclear as they would from the cast hexagram, and even the World of Thought nuclear can be read to give one some further insight to what is/was going on behind the scenes to cause such an occurrence in the present time.

There is always more and more information available from the I Ching Oracle, but *we **must** remember that we are very limited in our ability to interpret and can become very muddled indeed.*

I personally did not start using nuclears until I felt absolutely confident with what I already had achieved.

Chapter 5
Casting a Hexagram
The How's, Why's, Wherefore's
Examples of Readings
How to Use the Chart to Locate the Cast Hexagram

A cast is made six times with three coins. This gives six lines written from the bottom up, making a hexagram and showing two trigrams one above the other. The coins themselves should be round (heaven, encompassing), usually with a small open square in the middle (earth, receptive.) One side is usually patterned, the other plain. The user decides which side to call Yin, which side Yang and thereafter they must never be reversed. At each casting the total can only be 6, 7, 8 or 9. The **Yang** side of each coin is given the value **3** (representing the Trinity, Godhead) and the **Yin** a value of **2** (symbolic of the Receptive). Interestingly, in the 64 hexagrams, Hexagram 2 is called The Receptive.

If three Yin coins appear in one line, (a total of 6) (called 'Big Yin'), it is considered too strong or dominant, and becomes a 'moving' line. In other words, it is written with its opposite Little Yang (7), beside it and will be the basis of a second (future outcome) hexagram. If three Yang coins (a total of 9) (called 'Big Yang') appear in one line, it is too strong (too much heaven!) and needs to be balanced by its opposite Little Yin (8), so that, too, is a moving line.

Summary: **6 changes to 7**; 7 and 8 remain the same; **9 changes to 8**.

Example

If the first three coins cast are –

2 + 3 + 3 = 8 (yin + yang + yang) they would be written:

8: __ __ (no change)

but 3 yangs (9) would be written:

9: —— change to — — yin (8)

When casting the numbers are recorded from the bottom up.

Example

Top line: (big Yin)	*6 — —	(moving to)	———— 7
5th line: (little Yin)	8 — —	(unchanged)	— —8
4th line: (little Yang)	7 ————	(unchanged)	———— 7
3rd line: (big Yang)	*9 ————	(moving to)	— —8
2nd line: (little Yang)	7 ————	(unchanged)	———— 7
1st line: (little Yang)	7 ————	(unchanged)	———— 7

It can be seen that the 9 and 6 have effected a change, and the third and top line would be the two relevant lines to read in the situation. The reading of the first cast hexagram is taken from the World of Phenomena (action, the senses, present time). If there are **no** moving/changing lines, the hexagram is considered **'Locked'** and must be read very carefully as explained earlier.

There is a corresponding hexagram from the World of Thought (the cosmic activity behind the phenomenon) which must always be consulted to find the reasoning behind the present situation. This reflects the philosophy that the world was in thought **before** it was made manifest; therefore the situation thrown up by a cast had to have something in 'thought' to **cause** or bear influence on the present condition. We need to know the forces which made it happen or are happening. The World of Thought reading also indicates the ideas and aspirations, whereas the World of Phenomena demonstrates the visible things. It also scientifically represents unseen sound, light and electro-magnetics.

The World of Thought hexagrams have been derived from a diagram in Wilhelm's book and for your convenience have been included in Chap. 6.

As has been mentioned many times in this commentary one's approach to the I Ching Oracle should be one of reverence, respect, awe; it is a holy sage, a friend and has to be treated solemnly and sincerely. Furthermore it is this approach which also opens up the link between the sub/super-conscious and the cosmic, allowing more information, and of greater depth, to flow through in response to the request for help.

My own method is one of quiet meditation **before** approaching the I

Ching. Someone (or myself) has a question of great importance to them. Quietly meditate on the problem and question. At a given moment you will know not only what to ask but how to ask it. Settle and kneel, or sit quietly in a corner where you feel at peace and at one with God. **Write down your questions, always remembering the importance of the phrasing! Be logical and keep it simple.** Open your Book and address the I Ching as you would a great man of reverence. Hold your coins in one hand, and become familiar with them as if they were your lifeline to God; they are!

Bow gently to the I Ching and mentally thank God/Universal Consciousness for honouring you as a student. Pray for guidance and enlightenment. Hold the coins in your hand pressed to your forehead and repeat **aloud** your question. Feel at one with the coins and with God. Move the coins, as if gently moving them between the thumb and fingers (you will feel them turning around within your hand). Gently and without haste transfer them from one palm to the other, until a moment comes when you feel they want to jump out of your hand and on to the table/cloth/floor. Let them go. Quietly look down, read the faces, enter them on your paper **(from the bottom up)**. Again, with the same mood still with you, quiet movement of coins between palms, the moment to let go, the looking, the writing. And so on, six times. At the end, do not rush. Sit quietly, regard your numbers. Pick up your coins and place them in their special cloth/box/packet. Again bow to the I Ching and thank God for the link you have made. Pray to God, in gratitude and appreciation, and ask for guidance with your interpretation.

Quietly withdraw your mind from this atmosphere of magic and write down your lines next to the numbers you have 'thrown'. Draw their appropriate lines. Regard your hexagram. Now sit back, relax and enjoy the wonderment of whatever you experienced while in this meditative mood. Do not hurry to read your chart of hexagrams. The main work has been done; already the answers have been drawn into your soul. Your sub/super-conscious will take over much of the work. At a further appropriate time (if not at the same time) consult your judgements, images and lines. Always remember to note the World of Thought (what happened behind the scenes to influence the present situation) with its judgement, image and lines, and only when you are satisfied that you have understood the message and guidance need you look at the outcome. Here there are no lines; the name of the hexagram and its Judgement are the outcome of the present situation.

Warning! The I Ching does not tolerate fools gladly. It has no fear for its own reputation. If you are not of a serious and genuine nature, if you do not take your responsibility seriously, the I Ching will not answer you! Yes, you will have a response from the fall of the coins, and yes, you will find a hexagram to match; but invariably that hexagram will not only be nonsense, but might even cleverly mislead you. You have been sincerely and deeply warned. Do not play games with God's servants.

Would you tempt lightning to strike you? Would you taunt a river in flood to test your swimming prowess? Of course not. And so it is with the I Ching. It is your friend, your guide, your comforter, your confidante and the only one who really knows you and your link with Spirit/God/Universal Consciousness. You cannot lie to it; it will never lie to you. The opposite: When you ask a question you will receive the Truth. What you do with that knowledge rests with you. The I Ching does not criticise; but once a question is asked, remember that the more and more questions on a particular subject will **not** give a different opinion, but will delve further and further in to that situation, and may confuse you completely.

Remember too: the I Ching is literal. What you ask you will get. So spend time on phrasing the question and then the answer will be easy to you. **But it is more important to spend longer on how to phrase the question than on worrying about the answer.** A correctly phrased question will make the ultimate interpretation so much easier. Write it down before you cast, look at every word and change whatever you think might give you a confusing answer because you will be taken literally. So meditate, seek guidance and pray in gratitude.

Having received a satisfactory answer one should not ask the same question again; one should let the situation develop. If after much study the answer is not totally clear another question can be put, but **must** be re-phrased.

Another rule: Do not join two questions together. Do not use 'and' in your question; rather have two questions:

- please advise shall Mrs X visit America in July 1999?
- please advise shall Mrs X travel to America in July 1999 with Mr Y?

Note: The 'superior man' referred to in a line (I prefer the word 'wise') is used to indicate that this is how a wise person would behave (querant). The 'inferior' is a person who behaves badly.

How to Use the Chart

The names of the trigram family are written across the top of the chart; this is called the **Upper**. They are also written down the left side of the chart; this is called the **Lower**.

From the six lines cast, refer to the 'upper' for the top three, and to the 'lower' for the bottom three. By moving through the chart in this fashion, the number of the cast hexagram will be clear. For example, an 'upper' Sun and a 'lower' Sun is hexagram 57 on the chart and this is the hexagram to be referred to in the Book of Changes.

It should be noted that Wilhelm's Book contains two sections. In the front of the Book the hexagrams are explained in a simple everyday way and this is the section I used when I began my studies. Later one can move to the back of the Book where the same hexagrams are displayed with deeper esoteric meanings. This requires a great deal of intuition and practice but don't be afraid of it! It is a truly magical section to work with and excellent for developing one's intuitive powers.

A final word here: There are very many books available about the I Ching. Some are invaluable for further studies but some are concerned purely with fortune telling. Great discretion is required. You will undoubtedly find that the right one will fall off the shelf for you!

Examples of Readings; Questions and Answers

It is most important, in fact vital, that one prefixes a question with: 'Please advise' then **'Shall'** or **'Should'** not 'Will' or 'Would'. 'Will' and 'Would' are asking for a prediction of behaviour pattern. **'Shall'** and **'Should'** are asking whether the I Ching **advises** a certain course of action.

Example

Will Mrs Smith travel overseas this year? Answer: Yes she will, or no she won't, but there is no opportunity for Mrs Smith to learn whether it is the correct thing for her to do, nor to learn why, nor to find the outcome of such a trip.

Shall Mrs Smith travel overseas during 1996?

The first hexagram cast will indicate her present situation. The lines will give advice and guidance. The World of Thought will explain what is behind this present situation/advice/guidance and the outcome will show the result of her taking that advice. If the hexagram was locked, then she should not contemplate such a trip at all during 1996.

But it can be asked 'shall Mrs Smith plan to undertake an overseas trip in 1997?' Note the use of the word 'plan' which can be extremely useful in certain circumstances; but be careful: Mrs Smith could **plan** her trip for 1997 but not necessarily **travel** until much later. It would be preferable to ask 'shall Mrs Smith travel overseas in 1997?' If the response is favourable one could then ask the same question, replacing the year 1997 with the name of an individual month, or 'the first quarter of 1997?' and so on.

Mrs X came to see me for advice. She was desperate to have a child and had been trying for some 10 years without success. I asked: 'Shall Mrs X be successful in becoming pregnant?' The response was a locked hexagram 51 – arousing, putting in motion; keeping calm in the midst of upheaval. She confirmed that she had had traumatic tests but had been prepared to go through anything in order to have a baby. And looking at the World of Thought – hexagram 30, Clinging – one could see that she did indeed want a child badly. But the hexagram was locked and this lady was sadly going to remain barren.

Shall Miss X be happier if going to live in ..? (followed by the name of a far off country.) Hexagram 58 (Joyous) locked. The answer is obviously no. The World of Thought was hexagram 29 which indicates she was in a miserable state of mind (hence the question) but 58 shows that she should rejoice in what she has in the present time. Again a warning! Be careful with the use of the word 'if'. Avoid it wherever possible. 'Shall Miss X be happier if ..' leaves the sentence wide open for: 'if going to America' .. as opposed to .. what? We did not ask, so the alternatives for the I Ching to work on are global and unfair. Always be concise; think out the question carefully. A better form of question would have been: Shall Miss X move to ... in 1997?

A lady, Miss Y, asked whether a certain gentleman would have real significance in her life. I knew nothing of her nor of the background to the question. The response from the I Ching was locked hexagram 37 – The Family. The fact that it was locked showed immediately that the answer was 'no'. Hexagram 37 indicated that the man was married – as indeed he was. When asked 'is he married?' the I Ching said: hexagram 3 (Difficulty in the Beginning) World of Thought 36 (Darkening of the Light) lines 1, 2, and 3. Obviously there were problems in the marriage, as shown by both hexagrams, and the lines told the story.

The outcome was hexagram 48 so it was clear that all would eventually turn out well for him. (Remember: the question was about **him**, and **his** marriage, not about Miss Y.) Miss Y then went on to ask whether she could write to the gentleman. The answer was locked hexagram 13. Obviously not. 'What will happen if I write to him?' she asked. Locked again, on hexagram 38 – Conflict, causing opposition in a household.

The I Ching says: 'Two women living in the same household do not agree.' So the advice was to leave well alone and there would be a great deal of trouble if Miss Y wrote a letter. I am happy to say Miss Y took the advice.

Mrs K was suddenly taken into hospital in a collapsed state with an unknown illness. Within days she worsened. I asked: 'Please give a prognosis for Mrs K's present health condition.' The response was locked hexagram 7: The Army. She would not get better; the army (of hospital staff) was working. The World of Thought was hexagram 20: Contemplation; a halfway state. The nuclear of 7 is hexagram 24: Return or Turning Point. Being locked, one can deduce only that she was returning to somewhere she had been before, but not to her earthly home. The Nuclear of 20 is 23: Splitting Apart. Putting together the other deductions it was clear she would depart from her earthly body, which she did within two weeks. All the lines gave a description of her condition.

A much beloved cat was missing. The owner feared the neighbour's dogs and the following question was posed:

'Please advise shall Pussy (his real name) return to 164 Smith Street?' The answer was hexagram 38 – Opposition – lines 3, 4 and 5. The World of Thought: hexagram 6 – Conflict. In Opposition, we see 'two daughters live in the same house and do not agree' – two forces opposing each other. Another cat? In line 3 we see an ugly situation: the wagon is dragged back, the oxen halted, a man's hair and nose cut off. Not a good beginning but a good end. Pussy had obviously had some serious difficulties. In line 4 he was 'isolated through opposition' but met a like-minded man with whom he could associate in good faith. He was not alone in his difficulties. In line 5 'remorse disappears. The companion bites his way through the wrappings' so somehow Pussy had been helped out of, or through, the problem. Behind the scenes hexagram 6 describes the conflict which caused the situation. And the outcome was hexagram 9 – the Taming Power of the Small – and literally meant the small (cat) had been tamed. We felt he had either been taken by someone or had died. Alas he did not return. And line 3 in hexagram 38 was so distressing that it was felt better not to ask any more questions.

On a lighter note, I owned an adorable female Cairn puppy. When she was old enough I decided to have her mated. It was arranged she would spend the important three days with a stud male not too far away. On departure from the owner of the stud I was informed that Jessie would be taken to him about three times a day. During her absence I enquired of the I Ching: 'Please advise, shall Jessie become pregnant?'

The response was hexagram 35, lines 3 and 4. And I laughed aloud to read the Judgement: 'the powerful prince is honoured with horses in large numbers. In a single day he is granted audience three times'! The male had indeed sired many hundreds of highly pedigreed puppies (a prince indeed!).

However the lines were of concern: 'All are in accord. Remorse disappears' and 'Progress like a hamster (in the dark, in ignorance). Perseverance brings danger'. The Nuclear was 39 – Obstructions, Difficulties, Barriers; the World of Thought – 44: Coming to Meet (a sexual hexagram). Line 3: 'There is no skin on his thighs and walking comes hard. If one is mindful of the danger, no great mistake is made.' Line 4: ' No fish in the tank. This leads to misfortune'. The outcome was 52: Keeping Still.

Summing up then, everything was in accord with the time and there would be no regrets. We were acting without all the facts and somewhere there was an obstruction. There was no pregnancy, no fish (ovum?) in the tank, and this leads to disappointment. 'Keeping Still' showed there would be no labour and no birth.

When Jessie was collected, the sire's owner explained that she had been unable to complete the mating as my dog seemed too small. She had done everything possible, and apologised profusely. Some twelve months later my circumstances changed and I had to undertake a great deal of travelling by road. I decided to have Jessie spayed to enable us to travel together although I was full of guilt and remorse throughout the day she was in the veterinary hospital. When I collected her in the evening the vet told me that he had had quite a job performing the operation because she was so small inside; and added that it was a very good thing – for her sake – that she had been spayed because if she ever became pregnant she would die in labour. The I Ching had already said it all!

I think I have given enough examples to indicate how the I Ching responds to questions posed, although I will add a note about the variety of questions one can ask:

Health: 'Please advise, prognosis for Mr X health in 1996' and again for a subsequent and the following years, but each one as a single question on its own.

Ethics: 'Please advise Mr X's ethics' – no date, no restriction on the I Ching. Ethics are current. I once asked this about someone who wished to do business with me. It was locked on 'Splitting Apart, Fragmented'. I turned down the business offer, and subsequently learned that he disappeared with his partners' and company funds. (Please note that it is unethical to ask these sort of questions unless you are already apprehensive and need guidance/confirmation.)

Business: 'Please advise shall Mrs.Y accept the offer of a job from Z;' and again 'should Mrs.Y accept the offer of a job from Z.'

House: 'Please advise shall (or should) Mr. A plan to sell his house?' and a variety of other questions related to whether he should put his house for sale, in which agents' hands and so on.

Do please remember that the I Ching is guiding us on our Karmic path; that we should approach it with good intentions because we want to do what is right. The answers will be astounding!

A final note: When asking advice for yourself give your full name, don't say 'I'. I have found that it gives one that extra detachment and one can read the Book as if it were for somebody else. It also helps us to learn that 'we are not the body' – we are space travellers (mind/soul/spirit) living in flesh for the purpose of spiritual growth, to learn from it, and pass that learning on to others where we can.

We **may** only pass this way but once; any good thing we can do, therefore, we should do, for we may not pass this way again.

A Very Personal Experience

I wish to share with the reader my own first experience of using the coins. I was nervous, apprehensive and afraid. Nervous of phrasing any sort of question, apprehensive in case the I Ching did not wish to respond to me, afraid of getting it all wrong. I knew if I did not do it right I would not have a second chance. (My comments and interpretations are in parentheses.)

So I held the coins in one palm and studied them 'meditatively'. I felt that the 'stronger' side (with the most pattern) should be the Creative (Yang; value 3), and the gentler side, the Receptive (Yin; value 2).

I started to move the coins from palm to palm very slowly and said (mentally) to myself that I hoped I was doing the right thing. I think in my mind I meant 'doing the right thing with the practice of casting'. (Also in my mind was the picture of a dear friend of mine who had telephoned to ask whether I could use the I Ching to give her some advice, so I was also wondering whether I *would* be able to help her.)

I wrote down the casting as follows –

line 6: $3 + 2 + 2 = 7$		
line 5: $3 + 3 + 2 = 8$	Ken	going in to 'upper' Ken
line 4: $3 + 3 + 2 = 8$	over	over
line 3: $2 + 2 + 3 = 7$	Ken	'lower' Sun:
line 2: $2 + 2 + 2 = 6$	moving line changing to 7	
line 1: $3 + 3 + 2 = 8$		

So in front of me was hexagram 52 – Ken, the youngest son of heaven and earth; the mountain; a period of rest. Movement has come to a normal end; a state of polarity; an ending and a new beginning. (This is also the problem of achieving a quiet heart in its application to men. It is also directions for the practice of yoga; it is physical activity where the body is divine – t'ai chi.)

The Judgement (which sums up the situation; what one may expect of it and its chief attributes): 'Keeping his back still so that he no longer feels

43

his body. He goes into the courtyard and does not see his people. (He rises above his emotions?) No blame.' This is neither wrong nor right, but is appropriate action.

The Image gave an overall picture indicating the basic application of the hexagram to a human, social or cosmic situation. It is the mountains standing close together; the image of Keeping Still. Thus the superior man does not permit his thoughts to go beyond his situation. (Advice to stay in the present; achieve peace of mind, contentment, control.) It went on:

'The heart thinks constantly. This cannot be changed but the movements of the heart (thoughts) should restrict themselves to the immediate situation. All thinking beyond only makes the heart sore.' (In thinking about my friend I had allowed my thoughts to go beyond the question/situation I had written down. Thus: 'Makes the heart sore' meant I had confused the issue.)

The moving lines are the crux of a reading, and the advice and direction. Six in the 2nd place: the 6 changes from Yin to Yang which means change and progress.

'Keeping his calves still. He cannot rescue him who he follows. His heart is not glad.' (The leg cannot move independently of the body, and if it stops suddenly while the body is in vigorous motion it will make one fall. The same is true of a man who serves a master stronger than himself. He is swept along and cannot check the other in his powerful movement. Where the master presses forward, the servant cannot save him. This is what I read and understood from Richard Wilhelm.)

If the movement of the back is brought to a standstill the ego and its restlessness disappear. When a man has thus become calm he may turn to the outside world where he no longer sees in it the tumult and struggles of individual beings, and has that inner peace of mind which is needed for understanding the great laws of the Universe, and for acting in harmony with them. (The I Ching?)

Whoever acts from these deep levels makes no mistakes.

And remember that earlier quotation?: 'God brings to perfection in the sign of Keeping Still.' It is a dog, a hand; steadfast. It is bypaths, little

44

stones, doors and openings, fruits and seeds, watchmen, guards, fingers, black-billed birds (that grip), firm and gnarled trees (resistance), protectors. 'And of all that end and begin things, none more glorious than Keeping Still.'

Now I looked at the World of Thought hexagram 51. This hexagram of Arousing, Thunder, is the inverse of 52. (It is the mysterious place where all things begin and end. It is the attribute of keeping still because the strong lines have attained their goal.) 'When it is time to stop, then stop; when it is time to advance, advance'!

The lesson of the Image is that of restriction to what is within the limits of one's position; to be aware of limitations and be content with all the present circumstances. The guidance is not to advance too quickly but to travel slowly.

The 6th line in the 2nd place is indicative of a person who wants to save not only themselves, but any other they have allegiance with. (And could it be one who does not listen? One who wants to move away and take a friend? Someone who was not keen, but is now? Here was another hint that I was asking not only for myself but for my friend as well.)

Then I looked deeper at the World of Thought ... (the past energies setting the present hexagram in motion) ... hexagram 51: Arousing, Shock, Thunder. It is Chen, the eldest son who seizes rule with energy and power. It is a yang line that presses upwards forcibly. The movement is so violent it arouses terror; symbolised by thunder which bursts forth from the earth and its shock causes fear and trembling.

When a man has learnt what these mean he is safeguarded against any terror produced by 'outside influences'. He remains composed and reverent and 'the sacrificial rite is not interrupted'. Reverence is the foundation of true culture.

Six in the 2nd place: 'Shock comes bringing danger. A hundred thousand times you lose your treasures. And must climb the nine hills. Do not go in pursuit of them. After 7 days you will get them back again.' (What could this mean? Self control? In the Baghavad Gita it says that 100,000 fight beside Arjuna; that these are the features of his personalities and held wrongs. 'Danger threatens and he must retreat to the heights, (meditation?) inaccessible to the danger. Resistance would be contrary to the movement of the time and therefore unsuccessful.' He must accept his loss of property without worrying too much about it. When the time of shock has passed, he will get his possessions back without going in pursuit of them.

Having filled pages of an exercise book with these quotations and their various interpretations by Wilhelm, I felt I understood that the I Ching had certainly answered me. I had been nervous, apprehensive and afraid. Hexagram 52 (Keeping Still) described perfectly the method and way of casting; that meditation is the key to a quiet mind, and that a leg (or part of the whole) cannot operate alone. Behind this (the world of thought) the shock, arousing, thunder, perfectly described my apprehension and fear. But then went on to advise that there was nothing to fear, that 'he retreats to the heights and after 7 days will get his treasures back again.' This was excellent guidance that one should study the answers before rushing into more questions. And advice that the wisdom of the I Ching is indeed a treasure and one to be guarded well.

But there was more in store for me to ponder. After some five days of working on this reading, the friend about whom I had been concerned came to see me. She wanted to know whether she should leave her husband and what to do about the arguments between them. I knew in my heart that I could use the reading I had done, and that it applied to her marriage and what she should do.

It might be an exercise to look at these hexagrams 51 and 52, line 2 in each case, in answer to her question. I have not yet disclosed the outcome of the reading I did: it was (upper Ken over lower Sun) hexagram 18 – Work on what has been spoiled, the removal of decay. In relation to my own studies I knew it was showing me that through meditation and the achievement of a quiet mind I could remove the soiled and old of the past and move into a future where I would at last be on the path. In my friend's case she knew from all I read aloud to her that she could, by realising 'that the leg is part of the whole', remove the decay in her marriage by control of her emotions and a quiet mind. This is exactly what happened and they are still happily together today.

A further study of the two relevant nuclear hexagrams (hexagram 40 in the case of the first casting, and hexagram 39 being the nuclear of the World of Thought hexagram 51) gives greater detail on my then assumptions. I did not study them at the time, only many years later and they confirmed what I had intuitively summed up.

Chapter 6
The Sixty-four Hexagrams and their General Meanings
The World of Thought Behind and Nuclears Within

(If casting for career guidance the associations are given where applicable.)

The student will find it helpful to write the name of each World of Thought and Nuclear next to the relevant hexagrams in the Book.

1. **THE CREATIVE** (alternative: Strong Action. This is the most potent and positive of all; the creative force ever pressing forward into new and more perfect manifestions. Yin (2) is the opposition it meets. Yang is stronger and overcomes the opposition, causing all forms to adapt themselves into that which has decreased; Positive; Male. **WORLD OF THOUGHT: 52 KEEPING STILL.** (Nuclear 1). 1 is the hexagram of time and leadership.

2. **THE RECEPTIVE** (alternatives: Acquiescence; Resting in Firmness) This is the complement of the Creative; the most devoted of all things; Negative; Female. Yang (1) enters Yin (2), changes it and produces something. **WORLD OF THOUGHT: 57 GENTLE, WIND.** (Nuclear 2). 2 is the hexagram of space, responsive service (not taking the reins).

3. **DIFFICULTY AT THE BEGINNING** Hexagrams 1 and 2 produce something, not necessarily a baby, possibly a work of art, an invention, a new project. In other words results are produced as the outcome of heavenly inspiration entering the mind. This is also initial obstacles. **WORLD OF THOUGHT: 36 THE DARKENING OF THE LIGHT.** (Nuclear 23). 3 is the hexagram denoting kindergarten, midwifery; gardening, planting, sorting and checking.

4. **YOUTHFUL FOLLY** (alternative: Youthful Inexperience) This shows a lack of learning or lack of co-ordination, and is like a baby

which cannot focus or use its limbs properly. It also represents ignorance such as is experienced when setting out on a completely new venture. It is sometimes given to show we should not be asking the question. **WORLD OF THOUGHT: 16 ENTHUSIASM**. (Nuclear 24). It denotes teaching, youth associations, hostels and camps.

5. **WAITING, NOURISHMENT** This refers to nourishment, being the first thing for which a baby cries. Minds have to be fed, so do enterprises. Waiting, with the assurance that a blessing (nourishment) will come. **WORLD OF THOUGHT: 15 MODESTY.** (Nuclear 38). Remotely associated with death; old age homes.

6. **CONFLICT** This reveals contention and represents the confused mind torn in two separate directions. It also emphasises the importance of sorting things out right at the beginning, and to mind one's step at the start then things will have a chance to work out; otherwise there is discord from the start. **WORLD OF THOUGHT: 23 SPLITTING APART**. (Nuclear 37). The hexagram is associated with judgements, the settling of disputes, boxers and wrestlers.

7. **THE ARMY, DISCIPLINE** (alternatives: An Army; Group Action) This is the rising up of the multitudes. It can refer to mourning, but is essentially discipline. **WORLD OF THOUGHT: 20 CONTEMPLATION**. (Nuclear 24). It is the army, policeman, disciplinarian, the government, an unexpected emergency service.

8. **HOLDING TOGETHER** (alternatives: Alliance; Union) This indicates the bond of union between multitudes; Merging (like the tributaries of a river). **WORLD OF THOUGHT: 46 PUSHING UPWARD**. (Nuclear 23). Associated with irrigation, canals.

9. **TAMING POWER OF THE SMALL** (alternatives: The Taming

Force) This is restraint; the restraint to which multitudes must be subjected. Overcoming something small that is nagging; partially relieving a situation; influencing what one thinks one cannot change. **WORLD OF THOUGHT: 31 INFLUENCE.** (Nuclear 38). This hexagram also points to drought or a difficult child.

10. **TREADING** (alternative: Treading Carefully; Careful Conduct) This denotes the difference between courage and foolhardiness. It is conduct. It is the ceremonies which should be exercised and which are the natural outcome of restraint. **WORLD OF THOUGHT: 4 YOUTHFUL FOLLY.** (Nuclear 37). It also relates to veterinarians and animal work.

11. **PEACE** (alternative: Flowing) This shows good prospects for a marriage or partnership. It is a peaceful way of life (although beware of stagnation). **WORLD OF THOUGHT: 53 DEVELOPMENT;** (gradual progress to union). (Nuclear 54).

12. **STANDSTILL, STAGNATION** (alternative: Blocked) This is stagnation, obstruction, decadence, bad prospects for marriage or partnership. **WORLD OF THOUGHT: 18 WORK ON WHAT HAS BEEN SPOILED.** (Nuclear 53). In work: morticians.

13. **FELLOWSHIP WITH MEN** (alternatives: With Others; Companionship) This denotes a wish to expand and unite with others; human associations, brotherhood, lovers. **WORLD OF THOUGHT: 26 TAMING POWER OF THE GREAT.** (Nuclear 44). In work: communities in the country, e.g. Kibbutzim.

14. **POSSESSION IN GREAT MEASURE** (alternatives: Great Wealth; Great Possession (Abundance)) This shows cultivating union; all things come to belong; count your blessings for they are many (not necessarily material). **WORLD OF THOUGHT: 33**

RETREAT. (Nuclear 40). A hexagram of business, successful partnerships and achievements.

15. **MODESTY** (alternatives: Humility; Low Profile) This is humility. When people have something that is great, they should not become conceited. It is also 'keeping a low profile'. **WORLD OF THOUGHT: 42 INCREASE.** (Nuclear 40). It is the scales, balance, the Libra of the I Ching. It is weighing things, peacemakers, judges and decisions.

16. **ENTHUSIASM** (alternatives: Contentment; Harmony, Joy) Humble people are sure to awaken complacency. Repose in the absolute confidence that present action is correct. **WORLD OF THOUGHT: 50 THE CAULDRON.** (Nuclear 39). The hexagram of music and dancing.

17. **FOLLOWING/ALLEGIANCE** (alternative: The Hunt) This denotes obtaining followers; adjusting, adapting; quit the old ways; learn to serve (follow) in order to rule. **WORLD OF THOUGHT: 63 AFTER COMPLETION.** (Nuclear 53). In the everyday, it is the hexagram of rest homes, convalescent homes, district nurses.

18. **WORK ON WHAT HAS BEEN SPOILED** (alternative: Arresting Decay) This shows removing decay and stagnation; putting things right; righting a wrong or incorrect action; a service that is rendered by people. This can be hereditary or psychological traits. **WORLD OF THOUGHT: 54 THE MARRYING MAIDEN.** (Nuclear 54). In work it is dentistry; mending things.

19. **APPROACH** (alternative: Leadership) This is two people advancing together. A good influence which has not been seen for some time is approaching. People become great. **WORLD OF THOUGHT: 59 DISPERSION.** (Nuclear 24). In work it is teaching, hospitals, nursing, caring, looking after.

20. **CONTEMPLATION** (alternative: Watching) Contemplation (by

the great) of those who need their help; looking down; a view. **WORLD OF THOUGHT: 28 PREPONDERANCE OF THE GREAT.** (Nuclear 23). In work it is the hexagram of inspectors, surveyors, travelling to assess, a watchtower, hypnotist, fortune-teller, a prophecy, meditation, adoption.

21. **BITING THROUGH** This is overcoming obstacles to union. **WORLD OF THOUGHT: 13 FELLOWSHIP WITH MEN.** (Nuclear 39). 21 is essentially a legal hexagram and in work is associated with punishment, operations, accidents, the legal profession.

22. **GRACE** (alternatives: Adorned; Adornment) Union must be carried out correctly. To be content is more important than outward appearance. **WORLD OF THOUGHT: 34 POWER OF THE GREAT.** (Nuclear 40). It is adornment. In work it can be associated with dressmaking, flower arranging, interior decorating. It can also relate to someone concerned with their public image.

23. **SPLITTING APART** (alternatives: Destruction; Falling Apart) When union is carried out to the end, progress comes to an end. It can refer to a physical parting, or a parting in order to make a secure foundation. **WORLD OF THOUGHT: 32 DURATION.** (Nuclear 2). In work – woodcutters, car demolition.

24. **RETURN or THE TURNING POINT** (alternative: Returning) When things have come to an end, there is a return to the right way; a return to virtue, or happier conditions. **WORLD OF THOUGHT: 37 THE FAMILY.** (Nuclear 2). This hexagram is also connected with convalescent homes.

25. **INNOCENCE** (alternatives: No Expectations; Correctness) This denotes freedom from disorder. Whatever happens, keep calm and do what is right and correct. **WORLD OF THOUGHT: 22 GRACE.** (Nuclear 53). It could be connected to a nunnery or the church.

26. **THE TAMING POWER OF THE GREAT** (alternative: The Great Taming Force) This is an accumulation of virtue; the great

nourisher; being limited by the strong, by the creative force. **WORLD OF THOUGHT: 62 PREPONDERANCE OF THE SMALL.** (Nuclear 54). Connected with prisons, mental institutions and other forms of restraint.

27. **CORNERS OF THE MOUTH** (alternative: Nourishment) Virtue has to be nourished, and this hexagram stands for nourishment. It can mean money or a reward as a result of effort. **WORLD OF THOUGHT: 55 ABUNDANCE.** (Nuclear 2).

28. **PREPONDERANCE OF THE GREAT** (alternative: Excess) This is the process of excessive movement; an overweighting; too much of something; dominance by the mighty. **WORLD OF THOUGHT: 60 LIMITATION.** (Nuclear 1).

29. **THE ABYSMAL** (alternatives: Pits; The Perilous Pit) Extraordinary progress can lead to peril, and this hexagram, therefore, stands for the abyss, the pit. It may not be as bad as it sounds, but be true to the self regardless of the situation one finds oneself in. **WORLD OF THOUGHT: 2 THE RECEPTIVE.** (Nuclear 27).

30. **CLINGING** (alternatives: Shining Light; Brightness) When a man is in peril, or in the abyss, he will cling to something or someone. It is sunlight, it is flaming beauty. **WORLD OF THOUGHT: 1 THE CREATIVE.** (Nuclear 28).

31. **INFLUENCE.** (alternatives: Movement; The Unexpected) This is attraction of the opposite sexes. It is wooing, sensation, persuasion. It is an influence from without. **WORLD OF THOUGHT: 3 DIFFICULTY AT THE BEGINNING.** (Nuclear 44).

32. **DURATION** (alternatives: Constancy; Perseverance) A marriage or partnership ought to endure. This is continuity, long enduring. It is also getting oneself into a fixed routine. **WORLD OF THOUGHT: 38 OPPOSITION**. (Nuclear 43).

33. **RETREAT** (alternatives: Withdrawing, retreating, retiring, yielding.) Do not argue/quarrel with an impossible situation. **WORLD OF THOUGHT: 27 CORNERS OF THE MOUTH**. (Nuclear 44).

34. **THE POWER OF THE GREAT** (alternative: Big Uses Force) This is the power of the great, the strength of the mighty. **WORLD OF THOUGHT: 56 THE WANDERER**. (Nuclear 43).

35. **PROGRESS** (alternative: Advancement) This is advancing, making headway. **WORLD OF THOUGHT: 44 COMING TO MEET**. (Nuclear 39).

36. **THE DARKENING OF THE LIGHT** (alternative: Intelligence Wounded) This is being wounded, hurt, injury, restricting oneself, not seeing clearly. **WORLD OF THOUGHT: 9 TAMING POWER OF THE SMALL**. (Nuclear 40).

37. **THE FAMILY** (alternative: the Household) This is returning home. It may indicate a situation where the family can and should help. It also tells how each member of the family should be situated in their proper places: the father a father, the wife a wife, the son a son, and so on. **WORLD OF THOUGHT: 43 BREAKTHROUGH**. (Nuclear 64).

38. **OPPOSITION** (alternatives: Estrangement; Disunion; Mutual Alienation) This is misunderstandings, alienation, detachment, estrangement. **WORLD OF THOUGHT: 6 CONFLICT**. (Nuclear 63).

39. **OBSTRUCTION** (alternatives: Stumbling; Arresting Movement) This means difficulties, trouble, a barrier. One should wait for assistance. **WORLD OF THOUGHT: 24 RETURN**. (Nuclear 64).

40. **DELIVERANCE** (alternatives: Getting Free; Removing Obstacles) This is release, liberation and relaxation. **WORLD OF THOUGHT: 35 PROGRESS** (Nuclear 63).

41. **DECREASE** (alternatives: Reduction, Loss) This is the outcome of loss, a reduction. It can mean reducing the lower self to increase the higher self. **WORLD OF THOUGHT: 40 DELIVERANCE**. (Nuclear 24).

42. **INCREASE** (alternatives: Expansion, Gain) This out and out expansion and gain. **WORLD OF THOUGHT: 49 REVOLUTION**. (Nuclear 23).

43. **BREAKTHROUGH** (alternatives: Remaining Resolute; Removing Corruption) This is dispersal, outburst, resoluteness, holding firm. **WORLD OF THOUGHT: 39 OBSTRUCTION**. (Nuclear 1).

44. **COMING TO MEET** (alternatives: Subjugating; Encountering; Debating) This is a confrontation; reuniting; coming together again. It contains a definite warning about someone who may appear harmless but who will prove dangerous. It is the hexagram of sexual intercourse, the second wife, the other woman. **WORLD OF THOUGHT 41:DECREASE**.(Nuclear 1).

45. **GATHERING TOGETHER** (alternative: Gathering Around) This is a collection, a massing together, assembling, congregating. **WORLD OF THOUGHT: 48 THE WELL**. (Nuclear 53).

46. **PUSHING UPWARD** (alternatives: Rising; Ascending) This is sprouting, ascending, promotion. (Good men in high places) lead to advance. **WORLD OF THOUGHT: 61 INNER TRUTH**. (Nuclear 54).

47. **OPPRESSION** (alternatives: Weariness; Burdened) This is utter weariness, adversity, emptiness. **WORLD OF THOUGHT: 8 HOLDING TOGETHER.** (Nuclear 37).

48. **THE WELL** This is a resurrection or transformation; continuance of life or development; returning to the ground beneath; that from which all blessings flow. **WORLD OF THOUGHT: 19: APPROACH.** (Nuclear 38). In work it is a bank, a building society; that which dispenses money.

49. **REVOLUTION** This is a state of change; moulting, leather, skin; overthrowing; a complete change. **WORLD OF THOUGHT: 5 WAITING.** (Nuclear 44).

50. **THE CAULDRON** (alternatives: The Ritual Cauldron; Cosmic Order) This is a sacrificial vessel; a complete transformation of a person or circumstance. **WORLD OF THOUGHT: 10 TREADING/CONDUCT.** (Nuclear 43).

51. **AROUSING** (alternatives: Thunderbolts; Thunder (Exciting Power) This is putting in motion; the beginning of movement. Keep tranquil in the midst of upheaval. **WORLD OF THOUGHT: 30 CLINGING.** (Nuclear 39).

52. **KEEPING STILL** (alternatives: Mountain, Arresting Movement) This is a state of stillness; the mountain; desisting, stilling. (It can often refer to yoga and meditation.) **WORLD OF THOUGHT: 51 AROUSING, THUNDER.** (Nuclear 40).

53. **DEVELOPMENT** (alternatives: Gradual Advance; Gradual Progress, Growth) This is gradual development; maturing; a gradual progress to union. **WORLD OF THOUGHT: 17 FOLLOWING/ALLEGIANCE.** (Nuclear 64).

54. **THE MARRYING MAIDEN** (alternatives: a Maiden Marries; Propriety) Things come to their correct point of growth. It is life, birth, sex, death. It is also discrimination; a warning about a

situation of person; a partnership. **WORLD OF THOUGHT: 64 BEFORE COMPLETION**. (Nuclear 63).

55. **ABUNDANCE, PROSPERITY** (alternative: Many Occasions) This is the state of having become great; plentiful; enough for one's needs and a little over. However, this is not *great* wealth. **WORLD OF THOUGHT: 14 POSSESSION IN GREAT MEASURE.** (Nuclear 28).

56. **THE WANDERER** (alternative: The Travelling Stranger) The stranger, wanderer, traveller; can refer to being out of one's element; having no fixed abode. **WORLD OF THOUGHT: 25 INNOCENCE**. (Nuclear 28).

57. **THE GENTLE** (alternatives: Willing Submission; Gentle Penetration) This is wind. It is the traveller's homecoming. It is willing submission, gentle penetration, gentleness. **WORLD OF THOUGHT: 58 THE JOYOUS, LAKE.** (Nuclear 38).

58. **THE JOYOUS** (alternatives: Stand Straight; Joy, Pleasure) This is pleasure, joy; the lake that fills up. It is 'my cup runneth over'. **WORLD OF THOUGHT: 29 THE ABYSMAL**. (Nuclear 37).

59. **DISPERSION** (alternative: The Flood) This is separation, disintegration, scattering. **WORLD OF THOUGHT: 45 GATHERING TOGETHER.** (Nuclear 27).

60. **LIMITATION** (alternatives: Restraint; Regulations) This is regulations, restrictions, restraint. **WORLD OF THOUGHT: 7 THE ARMY.** (Nuclear 27).

61. **INNER TRUTH** (alternatives: Wholehearted Allegiance; Inmost Sincerity) This is having belief; it is inner confidence and sincerity. It is taking the middle road and avoiding extremes. It is honesty and

truth. **WORLD OF THOUGHT: 47 OPPRESSION.** (Nuclear 27).

62. **PREPONDERANCE OF THE SMALL** (alternatives: Small Gets By; Small Excesses) It is carrying into effect. The small get by. Don't fly too high or it will lead to disaster. **WORLD OF THOUGHT: 21 BITING THROUGH.** (Nuclear 28).

63. **AFTER COMPLETION** (alternatives: Already Across; Completion) It is the equilibrium or climax – as near to perfect a state as can be achieved. This is just the moment when things can be upset again so there is cautionary advice. It is a state of climax; of making things firm. **WORLD OF THOUGHT: 11 PEACE.** (Nuclear 64).

64. **BEFORE COMPLETION** (alternative: Not Yet Across) This is a state of transition. There is therefore no end, only transformation and cyclic change. **WORLD OF THOUGHT: 12 STANDSTILL.** (Nuclear 63).

*It can be seen that there is no such thing as 'death' in the I Ching, only transformation from one vibration to another. In other words there is only **Change** – nothing ever ends or finishes.*

To end this chapter, I would share with you a very beautiful and warm response given by the I Ching to me in the early days of learning. I asked: 'Please advise, what decides how the coins fall?'

The answer was locked hexagram 42 – Increase. I read only the Judgement, and I quote:

'Increase shows fullness of character. Increase shows the growth of fullness without artifices. Thus Increase furthers what is useful.

> *Increase. Decreasing what is above*
> *and increasing what is below.*
> *Then the joy of the people is boundless.*

What is above places itself under what is below:
This is the way of the great light.
And it furthers one to undertake something.

Central, correct, and blessed.
It furthers one to cross the great water.

The way of wood creates success.
Increase moves, gentle and mild:
Daily progress without limit.
Heaven dispenses, earth brings forth:
Thereby things increase in all directions.
The way of Increase everywhere
Proceeds in harmony with the time.'

Clearly the Creative Force decreases itself to give increase to what is below – in this case myself as the querant. This act gives joy to the people (who consult the Book). Furthermore the Creative Force places itself under what is below (the querant); and this is the way or nature of the great light or Force. It furthers one to consult the Book for guidance. The increase moves, gentle and mild: one handles and casts the coins in a gentle and meditative manner. One can make daily progress on the Path without any limitations. Heaven/Universal Consciousness/God dispenses wisdom; earth brings forth by putting this wisdom into action. Thus things increase in all directions, and the way of Increase is in harmony with the time, the moment, the Karmic Path.

This was an uplifting, encouraging, loving and moving response.

Chapter 7
Some Suggested Meanings of Lines

All the hexagrams contain lines which can be confusing. Years of study and particularly experience have shown what they **could** mean. Queries have also arisen with my students and associates; thus this chapter has been written for the serious beginner. .

Hexagrams 1 and 2: these have been very well expanded upon by Wilhelm. However, in hexagram 2, the Receptive, I have found the following:

line 1 – when there is hoarfrost underfoot, solid ice is not far off.

I found constantly that for 'hoarfrost' the words 'thin ice' could be substituted. Thus if treading on thin ice in any situation, one can know that the solid ice is not far away. However the questioner should realise that they are, in fact, treading on thin ice in their particular situation. In other words, if cast as a present-time hexagram the subject is in a tricky situation; if thrown up in the World of Thought then a 'thin ice' situation influenced the current circumstances.

line 4 – a tied up sack. No blame, no praise.

This is similar to a 'locked' situation. There is nothing to be done at that moment. 'No blame, no praise' means that this is neither right nor wrong, it's the way things are.

line 5 –Yellow in Chinese mythology is the most supreme of all colours, and indicates high spirituality. Similarly, hiding one's light under a bushel (correctly) is praiseworthy.

Example: I asked the I Ching where I could find a lost ring and this line was thrown up. Further enquiry showed that it was in my home. I knew I could not possibly expect to be told the exact spot, but was relieved to know it would re-appear one day. When looking through my cupboard the following summer for a sarong in which to sunbathe, I pulled one from the shelf and my ring fell out. The sarong (a lower garment) happened to be yellow, and the 'supreme good fortune' in the line was the ring's recovery.

Hexagram 3 – line 2 contains a wealth of information and should be interpreted sentence by sentence, slowly and carefully.

> Difficulties pile up.
> Horse and wagon part.
> He is not a robber;
> He wants to woo when the time comes.
> The maiden is chaste,
> She does not pledge herself.
> Ten years – then she pledges herself.

A good example of this line is the following:

A client asked whether, because her marriage was in the throes of dissolving, she should respond to the call of a male friend to go to him in another town. This line told the whole story: the difficulties had piled up and still had to be sorted out. The husband and wife (horse and wagon) were parting. The male friend was not a robber nor taking anything that belonged to anyone else; in fact he would want to marry her when she was free. However, she is chaste – she does not commit herself. But after 10 years (a symbolic cycle of time) she pledges herself – not necessarily to the friend, but certainly to someone.

Hexagram 4 – Youthful Folly. It is worth noting that this hexagram can be cast and locked. It is sometimes the I Ching's way of telling the querant that the question should not be asked. In other words, the young fool (ignorant) is importuning and the I Ching is metaphorically slapping a hand!

In **Hexagram 5** – Waiting (with the assurance that a blessing will come and that aid is on its way) we are shown the various ways in which the client is waiting.

- Line 1: 'in the meadow' is outside the main field of action, and could literally be outside a town.

- Line 3: 'in the mud brings about the arrival of the enemy.' Here one **must** get one's feet out of the situation to avoid the negative events in the situation enquired about.

- Line 4: 'waiting in blood' can indicate that the person/client is in a sweat (blood), or overheated and should get themselves out of the frame of mind – there is no need for it. Another possibility is that the person is waiting within the family (blood).

- Line 6: 'one falls into the pit. Three uninvited guests arrive. Honour them and in the end there will be good fortune'. This reminds me of a question for a client who was desperate to sell her house. This line indicated that she was indeed desperate (in the pit) but that unexpectedly three people (potential buyers or agents) would appear. Furthermore they should be listened to and their advice heeded if they give any, then all will be well. The three uninvited guests were a family who called unexpectedly to view the property, and they bought the house within three days!

Hexagram 6 – Conflict. The lines are well explained by Wilhelm. I would like to give a note here about 'crossing the great water' as mentioned in the Judgement. In ancient China the sea was indeed 'a great water' and something to be in awe of because of its vastness and their inability to traverse it regularly. Hence to 'cross the great water' was a supreme feat, an action to be admired because of its nobleness and daring.

A note to line 6 (top): A leather belt was bestowed for bravery in ancient times. There is a warning here that although one may have had praise (almost past tense; remember the top line is moving out of the present situation), within a short period of time it will be retracted and the person on whom it was bestowed could even have been reviled.

Hexagram 7 – The Army. This is also the hexagram of the discipline that should be imposed; it can also describe an uprising by a multitude – such as riots. The 'corpses' in Line 3 indicate there is deadwood or negativity to be removed from the situation in the question. In Line 5 one should look to see how many people are involved in the question and it will be seen that the eldest (or male) should be the one to take the lead, and the younger is carrying negativity which needs to be removed.

Hexagram 8 – Holding Together (also Union, Co-ordination, Merging). The Judgement is favourable and kind. It goes so far as to advise that one can enquire again. 'Look at yourself; question your ethics' (sublimity, constancy, perseverance). Line 5 indicates a misguided approach to whatever or whoever the subject of the question is. An example is given of how a King approaches game: he foregoes the game that runs off in front of him. We should be like that King and not chase after something that is unattainable.

Hexagram 9 – The Taming Power of the Small. This is a small restraint followed by success; overcoming something small that is nagging; partially relieving a situation.

The Judgement shows how a small restraint has success. 'Dense clouds' mean that the situation is not yet clear. 'No rain from our western region'.... the relief has yet to come. In the Image we can see that there is a hidden and strong movement taking place outside our own sphere of influence ('the wind drives across heaven') and the wise ('superior') man refines his own nature in the meantime.

The lines are self-explanatory but in Line 4 remember that 'blood' can be 'sweat'.

Hexagram 10 – Treading. This is careful conduct. It is a 'Watch out!' situation and is the difference between courage and foolhardiness. Without fail I have found this hexagram always to be a warning and a lesson in discrimination. All the lines are well described.

Hexagram 11 – Peace. This means good prospects for marriage or partnership.

- Line 1: There is a grass which when pulled up will not separate itself from the soil (sod) in which it was growing. This is an indication of those of like mind holding close to each other; at the same time we are told that likewise 'each according to his kind' advises that 'birds of a feather flock together'. This line was cast once when I had a health query for a client who had been told she had cancer; she wanted confirmation. This line explained it very well.

- Line 2 is best illustrated by an example. A lady running her own business found herself with friends in another town. Does she stay? Does she depart and try somewhere else? The description 'Bearing with the uncultured in gentleness' indicated that she was indeed with people not of like mind, but that she was with them out of their kindness and she should continue to do so (gentleness). On the other hand, she must continue with her plans (fording the river with resolution, not neglecting what is distant) – the light at the end of the tunnel, or her personal goal – and not listening to other people's desires (who wished she would stay with them permanently) but keeping to the middle way. Not an easy task, but the advice was sound.

- Line 3 is similar to the above: There is no uphill path that is not followed by one going downhill, and no journey that is not followed by another one leading elsewhere.

- Line 4 also came up for this lady. There she was, without independent means, staying with friends, guileless and sincere.

Hexagram 12 - Standstill, Obstruction, Decadence, Bad Prospects.

Here in Line 1 we have a repeat of Line 1 of the previous hexagram .... but not quite. In hexagram 11 it followed after the ribbon grass statement that 'undertakings bring good fortune'. In this it advises that 'perseverance brings good fortune and success.' In hexagram 11 we are advised to **undertake** something; here we are advised that we must **persevere** in our aims and purposes.

The 5th line has cropped up many times: 'What if it should fail, what if it should fail?' is a cry many of us carry in our hearts. Supposing our plans go wrong and fall apart? So we tie it to a 'cluster of mulberry shoots'. In other words, like a piece of cotton we hang on thinly to our hopes and beliefs. How shaky we are in our faith!

Hexagram 13 – Fellowship with Men; Human Associations; Lovers; Like-minded Persons; Universal Brotherhood.

Here we have fellowship with men 'in the open'; not disguised, not behind closed doors. And again 'it furthers one to cross the great water' in that one can take the plunge or undertake a great feat. 'Fellowship with men at the gate' (line 1) indicates that something at the edge of our understanding, or someone we have met outside the family or clan, is meaning something to us.

- Line 2 – 'In the clan' is *within* the family/friendship group.

- Line 3 shows us that weapons (feelings/talents/abilities) are hidden, and one pushes ahead of them without showing any of it. For a cycle of time it will be this way.

Hexagram 14 – This is one of the most beautiful and delightful of them all. Everything falls to one's lot and we must count our blessings for they are many. A superb example was of a lady who had just married. A friend of hers asked about the prospects for the marriage. Locked hexagram 14! What else was there to say? It was Possession in Great Measure – locked/unchanging – and would last all their lives.

Hexagram 15 – Modesty (Humility). This is a hexagram of ethics already existing within the questioner or subject. Line 1 (the beginning of action) advises without hesitation that 'a superior (wise) man modest about his modesty (humble) may cross the great water' (attempt a courageous enterprise).

Hexagram 16 – Enthusiasm. One can have absolute confidence that the action now taken is the correct one. After, and together with, modesty and humility follows Enthusiasm. But there is a warning that too much enthusiasm can lead to inertia.

- Line 1: 'Enthusiasm that expresses itself brings misfortune.' It is wiser and more appropriate to keep one's enthusiasm/excitement for a project or circumstance to oneself.

- In Line 2 we are advised to be as 'firm as a rock' within ourselves about what we are enthusiastic about, and before a day (or short period of time) is over we will see the fruits of it.

- Then Line 3 in the place of present-time advises to still keep that enthusiasm to oneself; that we should not look to anyone else for confirmation of our inner feelings. And that to hesitate in our hearts will bring remorse or regret.

- Then here in the 4th line we are told that we ourselves are now the source of enthusiasm and great things can be achieved. Furthermore we must continue to doubt nothing. 'You gather friends around you as a hair clasp gathers hair' – helpers and trustworthy friends will come and join us in our enterprise.

- Line 5 tells us that we have had enthusiasm in the wrong place, and persistently, but we have not learnt from it nor given up the idea. But we should certainly do so.

- And in the top line we were deluded but if we stop now, give it up neatly and tidily, there will be no blame, no sorrow, no remorse. The top line moving out of the situation indicates our ability to achieve this quite rapidly.

Hexagram 17 – Following; Allegiance; According with; Adjusting; Quitting old ways; Learning to serve in order to rule.

- Lines 2 and 3 could perhaps be expanded upon as they seem to be trying to say similar things. It should be remembered first of all that line 2 is a weak line; the line is an admonition to let go of small, petty little things so as to strengthen one's character. 'If one clings to the little boy,' I Ching says, 'one loses the strong man.'

- Line 3 takes this a stage further: 'If one clings to the strong man' (holds to one's inner strength) 'one loses the little boy' (automatically).'Through following one finds what one seeks' – through loyalty, devotion, inner strength and purpose, one finds the path, the goal.

- Finally in line 6 we find the reward for our devotion: the King (the ruler, the saviour, the Lord) introduces us to the Western Mountain – the place of Kings, our goal, our path, Karma, the place where good rains come from to succour us after a drought.

Hexagram 18 – Work on what has been spoiled. This is the removal of decay; undertakings; service to a cause; putting something right.

When this hexagram is cast it shows without doubt that there is a stagnating/decaying situation existing and the lines advise what should be done to remove it. The Judgement gives the greatest clue: To work on something brings supreme success. It furthers one to undertake a great feat in doing this. However there will be a (short) period of time (three days) before one can actually get the work moving, and a short period afterwards before one sees any fruits from that labour.

- Line 1: 'Setting right what has been spoiled by the father' or a dominant person; or a situation which disturbed our equilibrium. However, if there is a son, in other words something came out of that situation – if we have learnt a little something from it – then it was correct and no blame should be put onto that situation or circumstance. It caused danger – a threat to our demeanour or well-being but in the end 'good fortune'.

- Lines 2, 3, 4 and 5 can now be interpreted in a similar vein.

- At the top we are advised, that 'he does not serve kings and princes'; he does not work only for the 'now' but for the greater cause of the brotherhood of Man.

Hexagram 19 – Approach. This shows two people advancing together or two concepts. Here the Brotherhood of Man concept is expanded. The Image shows us that 'the superior (wise) man is inexhaustible in his will to teach, and without limits in his tolerance and protection of the people'.

- Lines 1 to 6 are very well defined by Wilhelm and I have not experienced any problems in interpretation..

Hexagram 20 – Contemplation. This is symbolised as a ruler looking down on his subjects and the subjects looking up to him.

This is a time of pausing, of meditation.

- Line 1 cautions that the wise man does not pause and contemplate in a childish way. This is humiliating, although for an unwise man this would be appropriate behaviour. We must take a more mature stance.

- Line 2 indicates that one has been looking at the problem or situation in a small, narrow way (a crack in the door), and probably leaning on one's weaker nature.

- In Line 3 we learn that all is not lost. We look at where we are positioned and then make our choices. The remaining lines are self-explanatory.

Note: This can sometimes indicate that we have reached a halfway mark or that we are half-right in our question. For example: Should Mr X move his business to situation A? Hexagram 20: perhaps some of it, not all. There is certainly food for thought. Depending on the individual lines we must not be hasty in our actions. Remember too: The Kings of old walked towards the gate – they regarded their people and their people looked up to them. Both were in a contemplative state.

Hexagram 21 – Biting Through. This indicates overcoming obstacles to union. It is a legal hexagram.

Having meditated (hexagram 20) and made our choices we are now in a position to decide what steps we take next. The lines tell their own story of the situation we find ourselves in.

- In line 1 there is nothing we can do; our feet are held fast but there is 'no blame'. This means that it is not inappropriate that we are in this position. The fact that we can do nothing is without mistake.

- In line 2 we, or the situation, have gone a little too far but if we realise this there is no need for further chastisement.

- In line 3 there was, or is something wrong. Did we dig up something from the past (old dried meat) that came back at us in a (poisonous) negative way? There was slight humiliation but again 'no blame'.

- In line 4 the meat is gristly, unchewable and certainly not to our liking nor beneficial to our success. But there is help at hand (metal arrows). It is in our interest to be mindful of the difficulties and to persevere.

- Line 5 is clearly explained.

- Line 6 (moving out of the situation) shows that there has been a rigid, stiff-necked attitude preventing one from taking anyone else's advice.

Hexagram 22 – Grace, Elegance

Here are guide-lines for our conduct and ethics, and the Image describes the intention of the hexagram that the wise man behaves with elegance when attending to current, everyday affairs although in anything of a controversial nature he must seek further advice.

- In line 4 'grace or simplicity?' is plain enough; a caution and a question as to our intent. I have always had some difficulty with 'a white horse comes as if on wings' because white is the colour of mourning in China. However, I have also found 'a knight in shining armour' to be an appropriate interpretation, who comes not as a robber but as a friend.

- The 5th line's 'roll of silk' pertains to one's possession, or to an item to which the original question referred and a description thereof. This is something slightly humiliating at the time but all's well eventually. It shows that the tools at one's disposal in this situation are not equal to the task.

Hexagram 23 – Splitting Apart. (Fracturing; peeling off; breaking in order to make a secure foundation)

- Lines 1, 2 and 4 give the symbol of a bed as being the foundation. If 'the leg' is split it is in a shaky state and to persevere with it brings ruin – it must end. When 'split at the edge' one is totally alone without a comrade.

- In Line 3 he splits with them altogether.

- Moving into line 5 the situation has shifted into the positive, and the top line (the ruler) assures us that something hidden and full of goodness is coming; those who are against us fall completely away and the superior/wise man receives a motivation. This comes to him; he does not have to go looking for it.

Hexagram 24 – Return. (The turning point; return to happier conditions; returning to where one has lived/loved/worked before)

In the previous hexagram we moved through total negativity into hope for the future. Now we are shown how these changes are coming about and what action to take. We are back in the light.

- Lines 1 to 5 guide us well and in every instance 'without blame', 'no remorse' and 'good fortune'.

- Line 6 is not good; we missed an opportunity and suffered (or acted) incorrectly both within ourselves and with the outside conditions we were trying to change. We must know that it would be disastrous to use that method – for a long period of time we would not be able to get back on our feet/overcome that situation.

Hexagram 25 – Innocence (Integrity; keep calm and do what is right; an unexpected influence from without)

There is nothing to add to Wilhelm's notes on this hexagram.

Hexagram 26 – The Taming Power of the Great (The great nourisher; holding firm)

There is a restriction here but a very positive one. It shows great character and the strengthening of character.

- Line 1 is self-explanatory.

- Line 2 - one cannot move (the axle-trees are gone) even if one wanted to.

- In line 3 I am reminded of Arjuna in the Baghavad Gita: chariot-driving is a test of character and armed defence is our ethical standard. We should look to both.

- In line 4: 'the headboard of a young bull' restricts what might have attacked or harmed us.

- In line 5 similarly, and in the top line, we are released from a situation or free to act.

Hexagram 27 – Nourishment. (This sometimes means money as a result of effort.)

- The 'magic tortoise' in line 1 is truly relevant. The lines on the backs of tortoise-shells were used by the Sages of old as guides. As such

71

they were regarded as precious. To let 'the magic tortoise go' tells us in no uncertain terms that we missed a golden opportunity and we know it; or we lost our faith otherwise we would not have asked.

The 'summit' means 'elsewhere'.

- In line 2 it is wrong to look there, in line 4 is it not. In the latter the querant is shown to be 'spying about with sharp eyes like a tiger with insatiable craving' which is without blame and correct action.

Hexagram 28 – Preponderance of the Great. (This is excess; the peak; dominance by the mighty; too much of something; an over-weighted situation.)

From the Judgement we learn that everything is too much, too heavy and has reached its peak. From the Image we learn that we must be undaunted and unconcerned. Out of bad comes good.

- Line 1 is beautifully explained by Wilhelm, Confucius and Jung in Wilhelm's Book.

- Looking at line 2 we are advised that a new shoot/enterprise is sprouting from something we thought was dry, and that something that has gone before – 'an older man takes a young wife' – something new beginning to come in: a shoot. This is all to the good.

- In line 3 everything has gone too far and is disastrous.

- In line 4 the situation was given support before it broke down completely, but the motives for doing so must be pure.

- Line 5 gives the symbol of the poplar again but this time it is putting forth flowers – an immediate flourishing of an old enterprise/condition. 'An older woman takes a husband' – this is neither right nor wrong but accords with the time.

- Line 6 at the top: one has to go through the present negative conditions, and it is all rather too much for one, but although this is unfortunate it accords with the time. This could be seen as part of one's Karma/Destiny.

Hexagram 29 – the Abysmal

Having been in an over-weighted situation in the previous hexagram, a natural progression from there is to fall into a pit, or be in something over one's head. However, this hexagram may not be as bad as it sounds, and whatever happens, one should remain true to oneself – to one's ethical standards. This is a time of great challenge, and lines 1, 2 and 3 take us through the situation.

- Line 4 gives an image of one in almost straightened circumstances but with someone there to hand us the simple foods/tools. We are not given bread and water, but wine and rice! How blessed we are indeed!

- Line 5 gives hope.

- Line 6 has gone over the top and is in dire straits altogether.

Hexagram 30 – the Clinging; Brightness; Fire

This is a truly feminine hexagram hence 'care of the cow brings good fortune' – caring for the feminine, for the Yin.

- Line 1: 'The footprints run crisscross' (running hither and thither, back and forth), 'if one is seriously intent (of good intention) no blame.' So there might be confusion for the questioner, or the subject of the question, but if they are well-intentioned it is not blameworthy.

- Line 2: 'Yellow light. Supreme good fortune'. Here we have the colour yellow (again), a most spiritual and kindly colour and a symbol of the middle path or way. This is balance.

- Line 3: 'In the light of the setting sun, men either beat the pot and sing, or loudly bewail the approach of old age.' The 'misfortune' comes because here there are extremes of behaviour – no balance.

- Line 4: 'Its coming is sudden; it flames up, dies down, is thrown away'. Something that comes suddenly into one's life, or into the picture, flares up quickly, and just as quickly goes away, or was found to be meaningless. This could be symbolic of a sudden love affair that is passionate and short. The I Ching has made no comment on it; it was an event that occurred, that is all.

- Line 5: 'Tears in floods, sighing and lamenting.' An 'oh-woe-is-me' situation, full of regret; but 'good fortune' is appended to it which shows us that this was the correct form of action.

- Line 6: 'The king uses him to march forth and chastise' – the subject of the question is being used Karmically to take action. He has vigour and a high degree of intelligence and thus his achievements are great. 'Then it is best to kill the leaders and take captive the followers. No blame.' This brings the condition to its correct and proper state.

Hexagram 31 – Persuasion, attraction, influence

Note: The influence can be from an outside source.

- Line 1: 'The influence shows itself in the big toe'; things are **just** beginning to move. The influence is just beginning to be felt and the movement is intimating an outward movement.

- Line 2: 'The influence shows itself in the calves of the legs. Misfortune. Tarrying brings good fortune.' Here we wish to make a strong step forward (with the calves of the legs) but we are told this is incorrect and will not work.

- Line 3: 'The influence shows itself in the thighs. Holds to that which follows it. To continue is humiliating.'. We are attracted outwards; this can be sexual. But it indicates that we are influenced for the wrong reasons and this should be discontinued. We should be influenced spiritually not emotionally.

- Line 4: 'Perseverance brings good fortune. Remorse disappears. If a man is agitated in mind, and his thoughts go hither and thither, only those friends on whom he fixes his conscious thoughts will follow.' Clearly we are encouraged to press ahead with the issue. However we must remember that agitation or an unquiet mind will not be conducive to solving our problem and only our closest friends will stick with us.

- Line 5: 'The influence shows itself in the back of the neck. No remorse.' Again a positive line. We remain stiff-necked and strong. This can apply to meditation and I have also known it cast for health problems pertaining to the neck area.

- Line 6: 'The influence shows itself in the jaws, cheeks, and tongue.' There is no indication of positivity or negativity here; it is a statement of fact. It can apply to someone who talks unusually much. It can mean that we **should** be talking about whatever the problem is in order to gain some help. And in health it applies to the area quoted.

Hexagram 32 – Duration; that which is long-lasting; that which is continuing, and will continue to do so. This can refer to a marriage or relationship.

The wise man does not change direction. He continues with what is – it accords with Heaven (Karma). The lines are all self-explanatory.

Hexagram 33 – Retreat; withdrawal

Overall the general advice is that we are in a position of difficulty and surrounded by adversaries. The inferior persons must be kept at bay – with reserve not anger – and the lines explain how and why.

- Line 1: 'At the tail in retreat. This is dangerous. One must not undertake anything.' Don't turn tail and run. (If this appears in the World of Thought it shows that one *has* turned tail). Stand fast. Keep your dignity and reserve and wait.

- Line 2: 'He holds him fast with yellow oxhide. No one can tear him loose.' Here again the retreat is hampered. Maintain your desire to escape; keep to the middle path – yellow is the colour of the middle way.

- Line 3: Here again the retreat which has been halted is nerve-wracking. However now is the time to find helpers who will help us out of this dreadful situation.

- Line 4: The retreat is voluntary (again with dignity) which is good fortune for the wise man and which will destroy the adversaries, inferior elements and the negative situation.

- Line 5: 'Friendly retreat.' Here one can withdraw with friends and at the same time leave the situation with a friendly gesture rather than an evasive one.

- Line 6: 'Cheerful retreat.' Be of good cheer. It is better than you had imagined and you can leave or withdraw without any negative thoughts or worries. Go with a smile!

Hexagram 34 – The Strength of the Mighty; the power of the great; a great movement forward

In this hexagram, the wise man does not deviate from the established order but keeps to the proper path (or Karma; destiny). Each of the lines describe the difficulties we are facing and how to handle them. They are self–explanatory.

Hexagram 35 – Progress; making headway

The light rises up to Heaven and the wise man maintains his virtue.

- Line 1: Progressing but turned back, perseverance brings good fortune. If one meets with no confidence one should remain calm. No mistake. Here one is trying to push forward and is hindered, possibly by someone who has no confidence in us. But we must keep calm and know that this lack of confidence is part of the scheme of things. There is something better elsewhere, hence 'no mistake' (in meeting with no confidence).

- Line 2: We are progressing, but in sorrow. However we must persevere in spite of the sadness. Something is coming to us from the past (ancestress) or literally an inheritance.

- Line 3: Everything is in order for us to progress and we will. Sorrow and sadness disappear.

- Line 4: Progressing like a hamster. This is not the correct way to make progress. We are moving in the dark, and possibly in an underhand way. This will bring disaster if we continue in this way.

- Line 5: This is the ruling line and all is well. Our sadness disappears. We have no need for remorse about our gains and losses. We can proceed confidently.

- Line 6: Here we must not butt or push our way ahead in big things – only in the small. We must be aware of the difficulties and wait for them to be resolved. There is no mistake in this but downfall will follow if we take a headstrong approach.

Hexagram 36 – The Darkening of the Light. (Restricting oneself, or being restricted; hiding one's light)

- Line 1: 'Darkening of the light during flight.

  He lowers his wings.
  The superior man does not eat for three days on his wanderings.
  But he has somewhere to go.
  The host has occasion to gossip about him.'

The superior (wise) man (the subject of the question) is probably between jobs or journeys and is obviously unhappy in this interim. 'He does not eat for three days ...' He is probably without funds, or a permanent roof. But he has a destination in view ... 'somewhere to go.' Somebody (senior, employer, landlord) somewhere has reason to discuss the subject – not necessarily negatively.

- Line 2: ' injures him in the left thigh' – could be his wallet (certainly costly) or a part of the body affected by surgery, I have found. 'He (someone else possibly) gives aid with the strength of a horse.'

- Line 3: 'Darkening of the light during the hunt in the south.' In our search there is delay or aggravation. 'One must not expect perseverance too soon.' Patience is required here.

- Line 4: 'He penetrates the left side of the belly. One gets at the very heart of the darkening of the light, and leaves gate and courtyard.' Here one has found and overcome the obstacles and is free to go on one's way.

- Line 5: 'Darkening of the light as with Prince Chi.' Remember the history of the I Ching and the determination and achievements of Prince Chi who while incarcerated kept his inner light bright. One can know that one cannot be prevented from winning through.

- Line 6: 'Not light but darkness. First he climbed up to heaven, then he plunged to the depths of the earth.' Here one has gone too far, been too ambitious and completely lost the way. But being the top line going out of the situation this line's criticism can be a temporary admonition, or a warning to change before it is too late.

Hexagram 37 – The Family; The Clan

- Line 1: 'Firm seclusion within the family. Remorse (or sorrow) disappears.'
Here we have found help and security.

- Line 2: 'She should not follow her whims. She must attend within to the food.' Do not follow fancy empty dreams. Keep both feet on the ground then there will be success.

- Line 3: 'When tempers flare up in the family, too great severity brings remorse.' Going too far brings sadness. 'Good fortune nonetheless': good will come out of it. 'When woman and child dally and laugh' it can only end in humiliation. Is there some new project here (symbolised by the child) that is being delayed unnecessarily?

- Line 4: 'She is the treasure of the house.' This indicates someone or something which is deservedly held in very high esteem.

- Line 5: 'As a king he approaches his family. Fear not. Good fortune.' Here again highly respected and nothing to fear.

- Line 6: 'His work commands respect. In the end good fortune comes.' Both he and his work are admired and good fortune is inevitable, but not immediate.

Hexagram 38 – Opposition; alienation; estrangement; detachment

- Line 1: 'Remorse disappears' all sorrow vanishes. 'If you lose your horse (your possessions, job, lover) do not run after it. It will come back of its own accord.' It will return to you, do not chase. 'When you see evil people guard yourself against mistakes.' If there are people trying to hurt you take precautions, not only against them but against yourself making an error which would give them power over you.

- Line 2: 'One meets his lord (destiny, future employer, a person of importance in one's life now) in a narrow street.' This is not anywhere obvious and was/is probably an unexpected meeting. No mistake.

- Line 3: 'One sees the wagon dragged back, the oxen halted, a man's hair and nose cut off.' We have been stopped in our tracks, even reviled. 'Not a good beginning, but a good end' so all works out well eventually.

- Line 4: 'Isolated through opposition' one is alone but 'one meets a like-minded man with whom one can associate in good faith.' One links up with someone with whom one is in harmony. Despite the danger and difficulties there is no mistake in this.

- Line 5: 'Remorse (regret) disappears. The companion bites his way through the wrappings (the obstacles are overcome) and if one goes to him, it could not possibly be a mistake.' It even brings blessing.

- Line 6: 'Isolated through opposition one sees one's companion as a pig covered in dirt, as a wagon full of devils.' One thinks the worst. 'First one draws a bow against him (we want to attack) then one lays the bow aside (we decide not to attack.) He is not a robber; he will woo at the right time.' This person does not wish us any harm; on the contrary good will come in due time. 'As one goes, rain falls; then good fortune comes.'

Hexagram 39 – Obstruction; barrier; one should wait for assistance.

- Line 1: 'Going (ahead) leads to obstructions, coming (waiting) meets with praise.'

- Line 2: 'The King's servant is beset by obstruction upon obstruction.' He is doing his best for the right reasons but is handicapped. There is no blame or error attached to this: 'because it is not his own fault.'

79

- Line 3: 'Going (ahead) leads to obstructions; hence he comes back.' He changes his mind and comes back to the right way.

- Line 4: 'Going (ahead) leads to obstructions; coming (waiting, returning) leads to union.' One finds the support one needs.

- Line 5: 'In the midst of the greatest obstructions (difficulties) friends (helpers, supporters) come (to help).'

- Line 6 – 'Going (ahead) leads to obstructions, coming (waiting, returning) leads to great good fortune. It furthers one to see the great man' (the one in authority, with ability, who can and will help).

Hexagram 40 – Deliverance; release; liberation

- Line 1: 'Without blame'; without any mistake or error. Totally in accord with Heaven/Universe/Karma.

- Line 2: 'One kills three foxes in the field and receives the yellow arrow.' One overcomes three obstacles; achieves three ambitions; and through doing so finds the middle (yellow) path, or is rewarded.

- Line 3: 'If a man carries a burden on his back and nonetheless rides in a carriage, he encourages robbers to draw near.' This is a clear case of pride coming before a fall.

- Line 4: – 'Deliver yourself from your great toe. Then the companion comes and him you can trust.' Free yourself from what is holding you back; remove the blockage in your mind, in your life, then the one (person or object) who wants to come to you is able to do so.

- Line 5: 'If only the superior (wise) man can deliver himself, it brings good fortune. Thus he proves to inferior men that he is in earnest' and shows them what he is really made of.

- Line 6: 'The prince shoots at a hawk on a high wall.' He aims for something high (an achievement, a position). 'He kills it. Everything serves to further.' He obtains the object of his desire and it can only go well for him.

Hexagram 41 – Decrease; loss; reduction

- Line 1: 'Going quickly when one's tasks are finished is without blame.' It is clearly quite in order to move on. 'But one must reflect on how much one may decrease others.' Be discriminate, hurt no-one else in the process, or take action to ensure there is no hurt.

- Line 2: 'Perseverance (in this situation) furthers. To undertake something (else) brings misfortune. Without decreasing (without any loss to) oneself, one is able to bring increase (help, assistance) to others.'

- Line 3: 'When three people journey together, their number decreases by one.' In a group or business situation, there might well be a break-up coming. But 'when one man journeys alone, he finds a companion.' The one left behind, or the one deciding to go it alone, will soon find a (good, appropriate) companion.

- Line 4: 'If a man decreases his faults, it makes the other hasten to come and rejoice.' A little soul-searching, or an apology, would not be out of place here, and is ultimately a cause for joy.

- Line 5: 'Someone does indeed increase him.' (Something really superb has been or will be offered to the questioner.) 'Ten pairs of tortoises (a holy symbol) cannot oppose it. Supreme good fortune.' The querant really is in the right place at the right time.

- Line 6: 'If one is increased without depriving others (not at their expense), there is no mistake. Perseverance (along these lines) brings good fortune. It furthers one to undertake something. One obtains servants (helpers, assistants) but no longer has a separate home.' One is no longer alone or without companions.

Hexagram 42 – Increase; expansion; gain

- Line 1: 'It furthers one to accomplish great deeds (in answer to the question). Supreme good fortune (it can only go well). No blame (no mistake).'

- Line 2: 'Someone does indeed increase him; ten pairs of tortoises cannot oppose it. Constant perseverance (in the way we are moving) brings good fortune. The King presents him before God. Good fortune.' This line is similar to but stronger than line 5 of the previous hexagram. Here it is shown that this is destiny and pre-ordained and not mere chance.

- Line 3: 'One is enriched through unfortunate events (good comes from bad). No mistake, if you are sincere and walk in the middle (take the middle path) and report with a seal (with honesty and integrity) to the Prince' (he who is in authority or in a position of (friendly) power).

- Line 4: 'If you walk in the middle (taking the middle path) and report to the Prince (see line 3), he will follow (agree, support). It furthers one to be used in the removal of the capital' – in the changes taking place within an organisation, company, town.

- Line 5: 'If in truth you have a kind (sincere) heart, ask not. Truly, kindness will be recognised as your virtue.' You will be rewarded and your purpose fulfilled.

- Line 6: 'He brings increase to no-one. (Someone within the question or within the situation is selfish, demanding). Indeed, someone even strikes him. (The subject in the question has an enemy, an opponent, a rival.) He does not keep his heart constantly steady.' (The questioner is uncertain, his faith falters and this is unfortunate for him.)

Hexagram 43 – Breakthrough; resoluteness

- Line 1: 'Mighty in the forward-striding toes (pushing forward with great strength and vigour). When one goes (ahead) and is not equal to the task (not adequate, not prepared), one makes a mistake.' There is no blame, nor good fortune; it is the way things are.

- Line 2: 'A cry of alarm. (One is apprehensive and nervous.) Arms at evening and at night. (His mind is restless and concerned.) Fear nothing.' There is actually nothing to fear in this situation.

- Line 3: 'To be powerful in the cheekbones brings misfortune. (There is too much idle gossip and talk.) The superior (wise, well-guided) man is firmly resolved. (He is not to be put off.) He walks alone and is caught in the rain. (He has no support.) He is bespattered, and people murmur against him. (He is caught up in the gossip, may even be the subject of it.) No mistake.' (Things are working out as they should.)

- Line 4: 'There is no skin on his thighs, and walking comes hard. (He is really having a hard time of it, and struggling against the problems confronting him.) If a man were to let himself be led like a sheep, remorse would disappear. (If only he would listen to sound advice he would not be worried.) But if these words are heard they will not be believed.' He does not listen, nor does he believe the advice to be helpful.

- Line 5: 'In dealing with weeds, firm resolution is necessary. (When rooting out trouble, setbacks, one must be firm and strong.) Walking in the middle remains free of blame.' (Taking the middle (careful) path keeps one free from further errors.)

- Line 6: 'No cry. In the end misfortune comes.' By not crying out, asking for assistance or help, misfortune will result.

Hexagram 44 – Coming to meet; confrontation; meeting; debate; sexual attraction; the 'other' man/woman; a warning about a person or situation which appears harmless

- Line 1: 'It must be checked with a brake of bronze.' Control must be applied firmly. (Bronze is a hard metal.) Perseverance (in this course) brings good fortune. 'If one lets it take its course, (without putting a firm brake on) one experiences misfortune. Even a lean pig (a person or situation which appears harmless) has it in him to rage around (cause trouble).'

- Line 2: 'There is a fish in the tank. No mistake. It does not further guests.' There is something in this situation meant for the questioner, and not for outsiders.

- Line 3: 'There is no skin on his thighs and walking comes hard.' He is experiencing a bad time and needs strength and courage to continue (in his present situation). 'If one is mindful of the danger no great mistake is made.' As long as he is aware of his difficulties they will not get any worse for him.

- Line 4: 'No fish in the tank. (Nothing at all in this situation.) This leads to misfortune.' If we persist in looking here for our needs to be fulfilled we will come up empty.

- Line 5: 'A melon covered with willow leaves. Hidden lines. Then it drops down to one from heaven.' A hidden luscious fruit just waiting for us. We cannot see or know exactly what it is but it will come to us as ordained.

- Line 6: 'He comes to meet with his horns.' This is a 'bull in a china shop' syndrome. The behaviour is humiliating and should be stopped but it is understandable nonetheless.

Hexagram 45 – Gathering together; congregating

- Line 1: 'If you are sincere, but not to the end, there will sometimes be confusion, sometimes gathering together.' If you are half-hearted and playing games with those with whom you associate (in the situation of the question) there will be moments of loyalty from others and moments when they withdraw. 'If you call out (to them with honesty) then after one grasp of the hand you can laugh again.' It will clear the air and create stability. 'Regret not. Going (forward) is without blame.' (Without mistake.)

- Line 2: 'Letting oneself be drawn brings good fortune and remains blameless.' If one has been approached to join (a project, relationship) this is right. 'If one is sincere, it furthers one to bring even a small offering.' If this is what the subject of the question really wants to do an offering on his part, no matter how small, will add to his integrity.

- Line 3: 'Gathering together amid sighs. Nothing that would further.' A situation where there are recriminations, regrets, it is pointless pursuing it. 'Going (forward, away) is without mistake. Slight humiliation.'

- Line 4: 'Great good fortune. No mistake.' Everything is as it should be and in good order.

- Line 5: 'If in gathering together one has position (authority, or something worthwhile to offer) this brings no mistake. If there are some who are not yet sincerely in the work (not committed or reluctant), sublime and enduring perseverance is needed.' (They need to be gently yet continuously persuaded.) 'Then remorse disappears.' (All occasion for regret is removed.)

- Line 6: 'Lamenting and sighing, floods of tears. No blame.' Tranquillity has gone out of the situation, one is left unhappily with regrets. But there is no blame in this; it is just the way things are. (Being the top line going out of the situation these feelings can be overcome.)

Hexagram 46 – Pushing upward; sprouting; ascending; often a direct rise from obscurity and lowliness to power and influence.

- Line 1: 'Pushing upward that meets with confidence brings great good fortune.' (He has support in his ambitions.)

- Line 2: 'If one is sincere it furthers one to bring even a small offering'. If one sincerely desires what is being sought, it will better his position to put something of himself into the situation no matter how small or insignificant it might be.

- Line 3: 'One pushes upward into an empty city.' There is absolutely nothing to be gained from this situation.

- Line 4: 'The King offers him Mount Chi. Good fortune.' This is a high award, a place and position of honour. 'No blame' – this has been well-deserved.

- Line 5: 'Perseverance (in achieving the object of the question) brings good fortune, but 'One pushes upward by steps' – it comes to one gradually.

- Line 6: 'Pushing upward in darkness (one cannot yet see the end result but) it furthers one to be unremittingly persevering.' One must continue pressing forward.

Hexagram 47 – Oppression; exhaustion; weariness; adversity

- Line 1: 'One sits oppressed under a bare tree (one has lost virtually everything) and strays into a gloomy valley (a depressing situation). For three years (a period of time) one sees nothing (and has no end in view).'

- Line 2: 'One is oppressed while at meat and drink.' There is enough for his needs but is in a depressing situation. 'The man with the scarlet kneebands (who comes to our aid) is just coming. It furthers one to offer sacrifice (to repent, make amends). To set forward (to take any action alone) brings misfortune. No blame.'

- Line 3: 'A man permits himself to be oppressed by stone. (He is allowing himself to be overwhelmed by it.) And leans on thorns and thistles.' (He is giving in to the situation.) For example 'he enters his house and does not see his wife': His mind is so beset with his problem that he does not see even those closest to him. This is not to be encouraged.

- Line 4: 'He comes very quietly, oppressed in a golden carriage.' He actually has much coming to him which he is as yet unable to make use of, or possibly does not even realise there is wealth available. 'Humiliation, but the end is reached.' It is coming without doubt and he must hold on to that belief.

- Line 5: 'His nose and feet are cut off.' (He is feeling totally humiliated.) 'Oppression at the hands of the man with the purple kneebands' (from someone in authority.) 'Joy comes softly (quietly). It furthers one to make offerings and libations.' An alternative proposition could be called for here.

- Line 6: 'He is oppressed by creeping vines (trapped in the situation). He moves uncertainly (he does not know which way to turn) and says movement brings remorse.' He thinks that whatever he does will not help him. (But) 'if one feels remorse over this (shakes oneself out of it) and makes a start (mentally) good fortune comes.'

Hexagram 48 – The Well; resurrection (of what appeared finished); transformation

- Line 1: 'One does not drink the mud of the well. (One does not dig up or live in the past.) No animals come to an old well.' No one is interested in it.

- Line 2: 'At the wellhole one shoots fishes' – one sees what one would like to achieve but 'the jug is broken and leaks' (one cannot hold on to those dreams).

- Line 3: 'The well is cleaned, but no-one drinks from it.' (There is something worthwhile there but it is not being utilised. 'For this is my heart's sorrow' (it is a matter for regret). 'For if the King were clear-minded (if he for who it is intended could clear his head of negativity) good fortune might be enjoyed in common.' It would be a cause for happiness to more than just himself.

- Line 4: 'The well is being lined. No mistake.' It is being prepared; there is a waiting time then all will be well.

- Line 5: 'In the well there is a clear, cold spring from which one can drink.' Clearly the situation has much to offer and one can take from it freely.

- Line 6: 'One draws from the well without hindrance. It is dependable. Good fortune.' The situation contains everything we need, and will not run dry.

Hexagram 49 – Revolution; change; taking up the new

- Line 1: 'Wrapped in the hide of a yellow cow' means obscured, hidden. (However 'yellow' is the middle path – taking the middle way – the path of least resistance.)

- Line 2: 'When one's own day comes one may create revolution.' The time has come for change. Action brings splendid success.

- Line 3: 'Starting (to make a change) brings misfortune. Perseverance (in this intention to make a change) brings danger.' (Don't do it yet.) But 'when talk of revolution has gone the rounds three times' (it has been well thought out and planned, probably over three days or a period of time) 'one may commit himself and men will believe him.' (One can make the change and it will be accepted by all concerned.)

- Line 4: 'Remorse disappears. Men believe him. Changing the form of government brings good fortune.' This is confirmation of the previous line, with the added inference that changing one's job, or place of abode, even one's current companion, is all to the good.

- Line 5: 'The great man changes like the tiger. Even before he questions the oracle, he is believed.' As the tiger moults and his coat dramatically changes, so the questioner will make his mark handsomely.

- Line 6: 'The superior man changes like a panther.' (The markings are more delicate, less dramatic.) 'The inferior man moults in the face. (The problem is dealt with.) Starting brings misfortune. (This is a difficult job to tackle to begin with.) To remain persevering brings good fortune.' Don't give up though; it will succeed.

Hexagram 50 – The Cauldron (symbol of a cooking pot); Cosmic Order; a complete transformation of a person or circumstance; taking up the new

- Line 1: 'A ting (cooking vessel) with legs upturned. Furthers the removal of stagnating stuff.' (The pot is upside down which is the right way to remove that which is holding one back.) 'One takes a concubine for the sake of her son.' One takes on this temporary problem for the sake of learning what is going to come from it; or because of what has already done so.

- Line 2: 'There is food in the ting. My comrades are envious, but they cannot harm me. Good fortune.' There is something coming my way which is just for me and not for anyone else. Nothing can stop it and no-one can prevent it.

- Line 3: 'The handle of the ting is altered and one is impeded in his way of life' (the way appears to be blocked). 'The fat of the pheasant (known in those days as the best portion) is not eaten. Once rain falls, remorse is spent.' Some slight action on our part – possibly putting right a wrong – will remedy the situation and: 'Good fortune comes in the end.'

- Line 4: 'The legs of the ting are broken and the prince's meal is spoiled' (there has been a disaster affecting us deeply). 'Misfortune' here states that this is certainly very unfortunate for us. It will take time and effort to remedy the situation. (A good example: some years ago I was trying to contact my son in England by telephone. It rang repeatedly for two weeks. I was concerned so asked the I Ching why I could not reach my son. It threw up this line but I failed to understand what it was trying to tell me. My son telephoned me eventually and explained that the heavy snowfalls had caused his roof to collapse. All his furniture, carpets and clothes were ruined and he had had to move out of his house until the roof and ceilings were repaired. The I Ching had explained it in a nutshell!)

- Line 5: 'The ting has yellow handles, golden carrying rings.' Yellow is the middle path of balance which receives the truth. Golden carrying rings bode well for us hence 'perseverance furthers.'

- Line 6: 'The ting has rings of jade' (very precious and valuable). 'Great good fortune. Nothing that would not act to further.' This is very auspicious indeed and we can go forward knowing it is to our advantage.

Hexagram 51 – The Arousing; the beginning of movement; keep tranquil in the midst of upheaval

- Line 1: 'Shock comes - oh oh!' (Something unpleasant shakes us and we can only say 'oh dear!') 'Then follow laughing words – ha ha!' (then follows joy). The shock brings fear and fear brings good fortune, enabling us to laugh about the matter.

- Line 2: 'Shock comes bringing danger. A hundred thousand times you lose your treasures (not literally; could apply to one's reasoning powers) and must climb the nine hills.' (This denotes a climb to regain one's sensibility.) 'Do not run after them. In seven days you will get them back again.' (If you have lost something worthwhile, such as a close friend, a place of employment or lost an item of value, don't fight the problem – it will resolve itself in due course.)

- Line 3: 'Shock comes and makes one distraught. If (the) shock spurs (one) to action one remains free of misfortune.' This is self-explanatory.

- Line 4: 'Shock is mired.' It is not clear; it has not touched one. Hence there is no mention of danger or misfortune.

- Line 5: 'Shock goes hither and thither. Danger.' It is all around one. 'However nothing at all is lost (it has not affected us.) 'Yet there are things to be done.' There is some action one can take.

- Line 6: 'Shock brings ruin and terrified gazing around.' We are not equal to the situation in which we find ourselves. 'If it has not yet touched one's own body but it has reached one's neighbour first, there is no blame.' If one listens to one's neighbour and remains calm, mistakes are avoided. 'One's comrades have something to talk about.' Our friends know about it, but we must be wholly independent in our actions.

Hexagram 52 – Keeping Still; meditation; desisting from action

- Line 1: 'Keeping his toes still. No blame. Continued perseverance furthers.' This means not allowing our itchy feet to take us forward. No mistake. But we can keep the idea in mind.

- Line 2: 'Keeping his calves still. He cannot rescue him whom he follows. His heart is not glad.' Again we must not go forward even though it could be something close to us that is in peril, and this makes us sad.

- Line 3: 'Keeping his hips still. Making his sacrum stiff. Dangerous. The heart suffocates.' Keeping ourselves still in the situation is dangerous, leading to heartbreak. We must most definitely take some action now.

- Line 4: 'Keeping his trunk still. No blame.' Restraining ourselves is the correct action to take.

- Line 5: 'Keeping his jaws still. The words have order. Remorse disappears.' There is a temptation to talk like thunder – don't! Think carefully then the words will have order and any regrets will disappear.

- Line 6: 'Noblehearted keeping still. Good fortune.' This is self-explanatory.

Hexagram 53 – Development; maturing; gradual progress (to union)

- Line 1: 'The wild goose (a symbol of conjugal fidelity) gradually draws near the shore (having been flying over water, i.e. a dangerous journey nearly at an end). The young son (a new project, an idea or relationship in embryonic stage) is in danger. There is talk. No blame.' This new thing will be talked about but there is no mistake in this.

- Line 2: 'The wild goose gradually draws near the cliff. Eating and drinking in peace and concord. Good fortune.' When the wild goose finds food it calls its friends to share – always – hence the good fortune attached to this line.

- Line 3: 'The wild goose gradually draws near the plateau' – a high place. 'A man goes forth and does not return' – he does not deviate from his path. (Or literally one's partner has left us and will certainly not be back. 'The woman carries a child but does not bring it forth.' If a lady draws this line it means that her hopes and aspirations in the situation asked about will not materialise. 'It furthers one to fight off robbers.' One should not permit doubts or negative thoughts to enter the situation.

- Line 4: 'The wild goose gradually draws near the tree. Perhaps it will find a flat branch. No blame.' A tree is not a permanent resting place for a goose; it does not have the feet with which to cling, hence it is temporary. But there is no mistake in taking this temporary refuge.

- Line 5: 'The wild goose gradually draws near the summit (where it is supposed to be). For three years the woman has no child. In the end nothing can hinder her. Good fortune. For a considerable period of time one has hoped for this thing, without success. But it is coming; nothing can stop it.

- Line 6: 'The wild goose gradually draws near the cloud heights. Its feathers can be used for the sacred dance. Good fortune.' It rises above the rest; it is blessed by God and all will dance for joy at its good fortune.

Hexagram 54 – The Marrying Maiden; marriage; business or personal partnership; second wife

- Line 1: 'The marrying maiden as a concubine. A lame man who is able to tread. Undertakings bring good fortune.' He/she belongs to someone but is not able to marry yet. The lame man is handicapped in some way (married to someone else?) but is able to tread (probably about to be free) and undertakings bring good fortune because they are able to receive each other.

- Line 2: 'A one-eyed man who is able to see. The perseverance of a solitary man furthers.' Again one is handicapped in some way but is still able to see and understand the situation. Perseverance – even if alone without any agreement – is the correct course of action.

- Line 3: 'The marrying maiden as a slave. She marries as a concubine.' This may indicate a person who wants merit which is undeserved. It is neither right nor proper.

- Line 4: 'The marrying maiden draws out the allotted time. A late marriage comes in due course.' There is a time for everything. If one has patience, what one wants will inevitably come at the right time – eventually.

- Line 5: 'The Sovereign gave his daughter in marriage' – the relationship is approved. 'The embroidered garments of the princess were not as gorgeous as those of the serving maid' – she was either second choice, or second wife. If the question was about business, then the questioner was the second choice in the situation or replacing a previous partner. 'The moon that is nearly full brings good fortune.' Things almost at their fullness are auspicious for us.

- Line 6: 'The woman holds the basket, but there are no fruits in it. The man stabs a sheep but no blood flows. Nothing that acts to further.' The woman has nothing to offer; the man cannot provide.

An empty sacrifice which is totally unfruitful. Do not pursue the situation in any shape or form!

Hexagram 55 - Abundance; fullness; affluence; enough for one's needs and a little over; many occasions; greatness

- Line 1: 'When a man meets his destined ruler they can be together for ten days, and it is not a mistake.' We find ourselves in or entering a situation which is where we are destined to be but it is not permanent. Ten days is a cycle of time and we shall complete the course intended for us. 'Going meets with recognition.' Going forward is quite acceptable, but we must not overstep the time limit.

- Line 2: 'The curtain is of such fullness that the polestars can be seen at noon.' We are blind in this situation but not so blind that we cannot see our polestar – the guiding light in the distance. 'Through going (forward) one meets with mistrust and hate.' One is doubted, not believed and therefore questioned. 'If one rouses him through truth, good fortune comes.' The power of inner truth and honesty will prevail and all will be well.

- Line 3: 'The underbrush is of such abundance that the small stars can be seen at noon.' The underbrush is like a thicket that no great progress can be made at this time, although we can see clearly where we are going. 'He breaks his right arm' (loses a partner, lets go of his prejudices, breaks with the past). 'No blame' (no mistake).

- Line 4: 'The curtain is of such fullness that the polestars can be seen at noon' (again – see line 2- we are not so blind that we cannot see our guiding light). But now: 'He meets his ruler who is of like kind. Good fortune.' Now help is at hand, from one who is destined to lead us onwards, hence the good fortune.

- Line 5: 'Lines are coming. Blessing and fame draw near. Good fortune.' Lines (normally hidden) are now coming towards us. Our destiny in this situation is about to be fulfilled.

- Line 6: 'His house is in a state of abundance' (it has reached its fullness; this is the peak). 'He screens off his family' (he is cutting himself off from where he is supposed to be). 'He peers through the gate and no longer perceives anyone.' He has lost his way. 'For three years he sees nothing' – for too long has he indulged in the abundant situation and lost the way forward. 'Misfortune' (wrong!).

Hexagram 56 – The Wanderer; the wayfarer; the traveller

- Line 1: 'If the wanderer busies himself with trivial things, he draws down misfortune upon himself.' Whatever has been asked of the I Ching here is trivial and should be stopped. Whatever the problem it is minuscule, so forget it – it is not worth worrying about or concerning oneself with.

- Line 2: 'The wanderer comes to an inn' (a temporary resting place). 'He has his property with him' (he has the tools of his trade, or inherent talents). 'He wins the steadfastness of a young servant' (possibly a young idea which will develop). This could refer to a person, depending on the nature of the question.

- Line 3: 'The wanderer's inn burns down' can sometimes be literal but usually refers to a place the wanderer finds himself in which is not the place for him; he'll either lose it or be forced to move on). 'He loses the steadfastness of his young servant.' That new idea falls away, or already belongs to someone else. Either way this situation is a personal loss.

- Line 4: 'The wanderer rests in a shelter.' Again a brief, temporary place; he has not yet found his right and proper home. 'He obtains his property and an axe.' He learns where he should be, and obtains the tools he requires. 'My heart is not glad.' The situation is unsettled and making one restless.

- Line 5: 'He shoots a pheasant. It drops with the first arrow. In the end this brings both praise and office.' He aims for what he wants, and gets it with the first try. This effort will result in praise and position.

- Line 6: 'The bird's nest burns up.' He loses his home. 'The wanderer laughs at first, then must needs lament and weep.' This is a matter of great sorrow even if at first it appeared a good thing. 'Through carelessness he loses his cow.' (He loses that which he treasured, which nurtured him in some way.) This is certainly misfortunate.

Hexagram 57 – The Gentle; gently penetrating; willing submission; homecoming

- Line 1: 'In advancing and retreating the perseverance of a warrior furthers.' One's will or faith is wavering. Here discipline and control – like a warrior – are needed to master the situation.

- Line 2: 'Penetration under the bed'. Seeking solutions or finding unnecessary problems in dark corners. 'Priests and magicians are used in great number'. One is consulting the oracle, or other sources, for guidance. They are used; they respond, hence the addition of 'good fortune. No blame.'

- Line 3: 'Repeated penetration. Humiliation.' Constantly pushing for results in the situation can only bring humiliation. Desist!

- Line 4: 'Remorse vanishes. During the hunt three kinds of game are caught.' Regrets disappear. We're on the right track. We find ourselves with three good choices, or three good people. This certainly has merit.

- Line 5: 'Perseverance brings good fortune. Remorse vanishes. Nothing that does not further. No beginning, but an end. Before the change, three days. After the change, three days. Good fortune.' We cannot go wrong. We did not start the situation, but we can see where it is leading us. There will be a short period of time before it actually comes our way, and another short period before we can actually grasp it.

- Line 6: 'Penetration under the bed. He loses his property and his axe.' Looking in all the wrong places we lose what we should have held on to. Perseverance brings misfortune.' Continuing in this matter will be our downfall, and the way comes to an end.

Hexagram 58 – The Joyous; joy manifest; refreshing joy

- Line 1: 'Contented joyousness. Good fortune.' One has found a way of inner peace. One has not yet become doubtful.

- Line 2: 'Sincere joyousness. Good fortune. Remorse disappears.' One has one's faith although doubt could set in. One's sincerity sees one through. It trusts itself, is sincere towards others and meets with belief.

- Line 3: 'Coming joyousness. Misfortune.' Distractions from outside stream in and overwhelm us with the pleasures they offer. This is far from correct for us.

- Line 4: 'Joyousness that is weighed is not at peace' (this is not real joy). 'After ridding himself of mistakes a man has joy.' After removing the obstacles that lead to joy we will receive great blessing.

- Line 5: 'Sincerity towards disintegrating influences is dangerous.' Trusting that which will ultimately lead us nowhere, or make us unhappy is totally wrong. Don't be drawn into something that deep down you feel is not right for you!

- Line 6: 'Seductive joyousness.' Here an attraction to some pleasures is drawing us into the situation in question and is actually base. Desist!

Hexagram 59 – Dispersion; disintegration; scattering

- Line 1: 'He brings help with the strength of a horse. Good fortune.' He is devoted and strong, bringing to the situation all the aid at his disposal.

- Line 2: 'At the dissolution he hurries to that which supports him. Remorse disappears.' In the situation where it appears that everything around one is collapsing one turns to those helpers one knows will succour and uplift. There will be no occasion for sorrow and one will obtain what one desires.

- Line 3: 'He dissolves his self. No remorse.' He is totally unselfish. His intentions are directed beyond himself. There are no regrets or any sorrow.

- Line 4: 'He dissolves his bond with his group' – he leaves his associates, thus 'supreme good fortune. Dispersion leads in turn to accumulation.' By this action he will gain more than he had before. 'This is something that ordinary men do not think of' – it takes a wise man, a rare man of vision, to see the favourable consequences.

- Line 5: 'His loud cries are as dissolving as sweat.' They are unnecessary. They pour off one. 'Dissolution! A king abides without blame.' He is in his proper place, hence without blame.

- Line 6: 'He dissolves his blood' (maybe leaves his family home, but certainly removes the need for bloodshed or sorrow). 'Departing, keeping at a distance, going out, is without blame.' Distancing oneself from the situation, rising above it, keeps one away from any peril or danger.

Hexagram 60 – Limitation; restraint; restriction

- Line 1: 'Not going out of the gate or courtyard is without blame.' Not taking the initiative, using discretion, and knowing when the way is open or closed is the correct path.

- Line 2: 'Not going out of the gate and courtyard bring misfortune.' One misses the crucial moment for action.

- Line 3: 'He who knows no limitation will have cause to lament.' One will only have oneself to blame if one neglected to impose the necessary constraints and disciplines. 'No blame': There is no particular judgement here. The line exposes the story within the question.

- Line 4: 'Contented limitation. Success.' One adapts oneself contentedly to the situation and thereby gains success.

- Line 5: 'Sweet limitation brings good fortune' (remaining centred in one's own place and even able to hold back if necessary). 'Going (forward) brings esteem.' Moving forward with this attitude brings praise.

- Line 6: 'Galling limitation' (being limited in this way is wrong). 'Perseverance brings misfortune' (putting up with the situation will lead nowhere and the way comes to an end).

Hexagram 61 – Inner Truth; inner sincerity; inner confidence

- Line 1: 'Being prepared brings good fortune.' This implies being inwardly serene. 'If there are secret designs it is disquieting.' There should be no ulterior motives.

- Line 2: 'A crane calling in the shade. Its young answers it.' There is a new opportunity being offered – although being in the shade it is not yet perfectly clear. 'I have a good goblet and I will share it with you.' The offer is full of promise and success will be assured.

- Line 3: 'He finds a comrade. Now he beats the drum, now he stops. Now he sobs, now he sings.' He is terribly confused. First he beats the drum of retreat, then he keeps still. Then he wrings his hands, then he laughs. These are all shown as symbols of the questioner's state of mind in the situation about which he has enquired.

- Line 4: 'The moon nearly at the full.' The situation has almost come to fruition. 'The team horse goes astray' (he leaves his own kind). 'No blame' there is no error in this.

- Line 5: 'He possesses truth which links together. No blame.' By his honesty and sincerity he draws others to him. This is correct and appropriate.

- Line 6: 'Cockcrow penetrating to heaven. Perseverance brings misfortune.' He talks or shouts loudly or boastfully. This is not appropriate behaviour in this situation. If the cockcrow penetrates to heaven it is a sign that he really has gone over the top.

Hexagram 62 – Preponderance of the Small; don't fly too high; a time of transition without going too far

- Line 1: 'The bird meets with misfortune through flying.' It is too soon to make any move towards change; there will be disaster if we try.

- Line 2: 'She passes by her ancestor and meets her ancestress' (this is shown as a symbol of deviating from the norm and being attracted or going to a wiser person of the same sex. 'He does not reach his prince and meets the official.' He does not make contact with the person in authority whom he would like to see, but the official will be quite adequate for his purposes hence 'No blame'.

- Line 3: 'If one is not extremely careful, somebody may come up from behind and strike him.' Watch your step with great prudence or you may be unexpectedly struck from another quarter. In other words 'watch your behaviour, and watch your back"! 'Misfortune' indeed!

- Line 4: 'No blame. He meets him without passing by.' This meeting bodes well. 'Going (forward on one's own) brings danger. One must be on guard.' On no account must one continue thus.

- Line 5: 'Dense clouds. No rain from our western territory.' There has been no apparent respite, but 'the prince shoots and hits him who is in the cave'; (he aims for what he wants and achieves it).

- Line 6: 'He passes him by, not meeting him.' He is arrogant. 'The flying bird leaves him. Misfortune.' He has flown too high and is unwilling to return. He loses his way and draws disaster down upon himself.

Hexagram 63 – Making Firm; climax

- Line 1: 'He brakes his wheels. He gets his tail in the water. No blame.' He calls a halt and finds himself slightly sullied, but this was inevitable/Karma, hence 'No blame'.

- Line 2: 'The woman loses the curtains of her carriage' which implies some form of window dressing, or impropriety; can refer to a lost item. 'Do not run after it. On the seventh day you will get it.' Whatever was lost here do not try to recover it yourself. It, or a symbol of it, will return by other means after a short period of time.

- Line 3: 'The Illustrious Ancestor disciplines the Devil's Country.' Again this is symbolic and shows that by honesty and integrity we can overcome the dark forces (negativity) around us. The Devil's Country is anything negative. 'After three years he conquers it' (this has been exhausting). 'Inferior people must not be employed'. We must not draw negative people towards us to help because they cannot.

- Line 4: 'The finest clothes turn to rags.' Even our highest hopes can turn to dust. 'Be careful all day long.' Be on guard.

- Line 5: 'The neighbour in the east who slaughters an ox does not attain as much real happiness as the neighbour in the west with his small offering.' Sometimes the greatest sacrifice cannot match up to a smaller more meaningful one. We don't have to make grandiose gestures.

- Line 6: 'He gets his head in the water. Danger.' He is in danger of drowning and only total disaster can be the outcome.

Hexagram 64 – Before Completion; a time of transition

- Line 1: 'He gets his tail in the water. Humiliating.' He cannot take the end into view. He has blinkers on and cannot see the wood for the trees. He does not recognise the danger of his position and so does not perceive the consequences.

- Line 2: 'He brakes his wheels. Perseverance brings good fortune.' He stops and waits. He acts correctly and should persevere with this attitude.

- Line 3: 'Before completion (before the allotted time) attack brings misfortune.' It would be premature to act now. 'It furthers one to cross the great water.' It benefits one to prepare for a great enterprise.

- Line 4: 'Perseverance brings good fortune. Remorse (regret, sadness) disappears. Shock, thus to discipline the Devil's Country.' This indicates a dramatic shake-up to remove the dust or negativity in the situation. 'For three years great realms are awarded.' For long into the future will we see and reap the benefits of our actions.

- Line 5: 'Perseverance brings good fortune. No remorse. The light of the superior (wise) man is true. Good fortune.' Extremely auspicious. After all the misery and heartache we are going to experience a new and wonderful change in our life. (Hexagram 64 line 5 in the front portion of Wilhelm's Book explains this most beautifully.)

- Line 6: 'There is drinking of wine in genuine confidence.' There is cause for great celebration. 'But if one wets his head, he loses it, in truth.' If we overdo it, or become arrogant, we will lose our opportunities for positive change.

And so the Book of Changes ends with opportunities
for new formations and new beginnings –
which leads us back to Hexagram 1 – The Creative.

Note: If lines are cast which appear conflicting please look at your question. I have found that if there is more than one subject the lines will be reflecting each subject's position. For example: A querant asked about the status of his directorship within his company. Three lines were cast but each appeared contradictory. It transpired that there were three partners and the lines were individually connected to each. One would therefore apportion a line to each individual within the company to interpret the reading.

Epilogue

I sincerely hope that this book has assisted you to understand and work with the I Ching. I know that once you discover its wonders and secrets, your life will never be the same again! It will change you profoundly.

Three golden rules–

- work out your questions very carefully, remembering you will be taken literally;

- don't intellectualise the answers, but 'feel' the symbolism of the lines within the answers in the hexagrams. Your Higher Self will guide you.

- don't _ever_ forget the World of Thought!

I welcome correspondence and will gladly and joyfully assist wherever possible.

Rosemary Howell
P O Box 23447
Claremont 7700
South Africa
(c)

http://www.gem.co.za/SpiritNetza/rhweb

Internet email _ching@aztec.co.za_
facsimile: 021-683-2344